Praise for
SWEAT MORE DURING PEACE
★ ★ ★
BLEED LESS DURING WAR

"A practical and inspiring book. Nick Cidado prepares you for the big moment before it happens so that you are ready to seize and dominate any big moment in your life."

—Jon Gordon, Fifteen-Time Best-Selling Author

"Nick's Cidado's impact on athletes has produced national champions, and the why and how is in this book. But the value of this book isn't only in maximizing your athletic ability; it's about finding mastery over your life. His book will leave you with tools to live with a preparation mindset, which is why I recommend this game-changing and life-changing book."

—Matt Hasselbeck, Seventeen-Year NFL Quarterback, Three-Time Pro Bowler

"This is a must-read for all aspiring athletes and coaches who are looking to gain an edge—informative, challenging, and hopefully the first in a series of books by Nick Cidado."

—Jerry York, Hockey Hall of Fame, Five-Time National Champion, NCAA All-Time Winningest Hockey Coach

"I have witnessed Nick Cidado transform good athletes to great athletes to unstoppable athletes by means of both his physical and mental preparation processes. He has crafted a culture of complete buy-in through passion, resilience, and discipline, which has prepared our lacrosse program to win championships. To be able to study his philosophies and intentions in this book will be a game-changing tool for anyone passionate about improving their journey to success."

—Acacia Walker-Weinstein, Boston College Head Lacrosse Coach, National Champion

"*Sweat More During Peace, Bleed Less During War* is an exceptional display of the life lessons I have learned from Nick. This book will not only help you forge a specific and successful path towards a certain goal, but it will help you build habits and a mindset that you will lean on for the rest of your life."

—Charlotte North, Professional Lacrosse Player, NCAA National Champion, Team USA Gold Medalist, Two-Time Tewaaraton Award Winner

"I can say with the utmost confidence that what Nick Cidado taught me as a young athlete directly impacted my journey to reaching the major leagues. This book will allow you to better understand Nick's philosophy on preparation and how you can apply it to your own life, just as I was able to do to turn my dreams into reality."

—Sal Frelick, Milwaukee Brewers of MLB

"Nick Cidado has crafted a game plan for success that can propel any coach, athlete, or team to reach the highest level of achievement in their respective sport. *Sweat More During Peace, Bleed Less During*

War provides people of all backgrounds and careers an outline for a healthier and more enriched journey through life."

>—Bill George, Author of *Home Fields: Coast Guard Academy Football Coach Recounts the Unfulfilled Lives of WWII*, US Coast Guard Academy Head Coach 1999–2019

"Nick Cidado's *Sweat More During Peace, Bleed Less During War* is a handbook of life lessons organized in a way to inspire others to achieve their own goals. Cidado offers up an array of anecdotes to showcase these lessons, creating a concise plan of action for anyone wanting to improve their odds of success in the game of life."

>—Carey Henry Keefe, Author of *A Tide of Dreams*

Sweat More During Peace • Bleed Less During War:
Preparation Tactics that Generate Success

by Nick Cidado

© Copyright 2023 Nick Cidado

ISBN 979-8-88824-207-0

All rights reserved. No part of this publication may be reproduced, stored in a retrieval system, or transmitted in any form or by any means—electronic, mechanical, photocopy, recording, or any other—except for brief quotations in printed reviews, without the prior written permission of the author.

Published by

3705 Shore Drive
Virginia Beach, VA 23455
800-435-4811
www.koehlerbooks.com

SWEAT MORE DURING PEACE
★ ★ ★
BLEED LESS DURING WAR

*Preparation Tactics
that Generate Success*

Nick Cidado

VIRGINIA BEACH
CAPE CHARLES

CONTENTS

Introduction: **The Beginning** 1

Prepare to Win: **How your approach dictates the outcome**

1. Sweat More During Peace. Bleed Less During War.....................14

2. Failing to Prepare is Preparing to Fail 25

3. Establish Your Preparation Tactics with Three Simple Principles ..31

Principle 1: **Get Organized**

4. Visualize the Moment 36

5. Start Right Away 43

6. Leave No Stone Unturned 52

Principle 2: **Become Disciplined**

7. Commit to the Process 62

8. Make it a Habit...69

9. Be Willing to Sacrifice 75

Principle 3: **Pursue Perfection**

10. Be About the Dirty Work..88

11. Aim High, Miss High 97

12. Get Your Mind Right...106

The Expected Result: **You only perform as well as you have prepared**

13. The Truth About Performance..116

14. Self-Defeat is Your Own Dispute 124

15. The Feeling of Accomplishment 133

Conclusion: **You are in Control**... 139

Acknowledgments.. 144

Prep·a·ra·tion
prepə'rāSH(ə)n

noun
1. the action or process of making ready or being made ready for use or consideration.

Tac·tic
taktik

noun
1. an action or strategy carefully planned to achieve a specific end.

INTRODUCTION
The Beginning

IT WAS THE first day of the first grade. Ms. Paul stood in the gymnasium holding up a sign with her name on it to congregate what would be her new class for the year. After being dropped off by our parents, each of us approached the sign where she would then greet us with enthusiasm and mark us on the class roster. She then escorted us in single file, down the halls of the school until we set foot in what would be our classroom. She then showed us around the room, which was filled with stocked bookshelves, extravagantly colored walls, and a massive classroom rug. She instantly made us feel excited about the new year and provided us with the warm welcome that was surely needed as we entered grade school.

I imagine this is just as much of an anxiety-ridden day for a lot of the parents as it is for the kids. For most families, this is the first time their child is consistently off on their own for extended periods of time. Parents must trust that they have prepared their child to be self-sufficient for the first time, and to understand that their parents are no longer there to help them. They must figure it out on their own, which can be worrisome. Ms. Paul, having recognized the daunting first day jitters, made it a point to keep us engaged and distracted while we connected with our new classmates and learned about the classroom. There was no time to even think about missing Mom or Dad.

She showed each of us to our desks before instructing us to unpack our belongings. As I looked around the room, I was intrigued by all the backpacks and the school supplies that everyone brought. I admired Anthony's backpack whose Batman theme caught my attention as he set it on the floor. Sarah, who sat across from me, placed down her Hello Kitty notebooks on top of her desk. Patrick, who sat a few seats down the row, whipped out his box of crayons and held on to them tightly. As I watched, the crayons remained in his hand, even while unloading other materials from his bag. He imposed what looked like a death grip on the box to either make sure that nobody would steal them, or maybe because he wanted to be ready in case it was time to use them. I couldn't help but notice that he also had the sixty-four pack. I was a little jealous because I only came equipped with the twenty-four set.

For me, I was especially proud of my backpack; I didn't even want to take it off. It was Spiderman themed, and you would have thought I was protecting it with my life, or maybe that it was protecting me. I dropped it to the floor, right beside my seat, and unpacked. I took out my folders, notebooks, crayons, pencils, glue stick, and scissors, and put them on top of my desk as instructed. I hoisted out my lunch box, which was also Spiderman themed, and brought it to the cubby with my name on it. My materials were officially emptied out of my backpack, so I retreated to my desk and waited for further instruction.

I was excited to officially get started. I had taken the bus to school that day, had all my supplies with me for the year, and had already been given the big boy talk a year prior, so I wasn't missing Mom or Dad. I was ready. That morning, I had walked around with the confidence of someone who had already been here and done this. You couldn't dampen my energy if you tried.

As I sat at my desk scanning the room while I waited for my classmates to finish up, I noticed that Patrick had a brown paper bag with what looked like something to be inside, sitting in the middle of his desk. I then looked around and saw a few others with either brown or plastic bags on their desks. I wondered what the bags were, but more importantly, why I didn't have one. It couldn't be their lunches, because I had watched everyone bring theirs to the cubby area. I also didn't recall hearing the teacher say anything about another bag, so I was very confused, to say the least.

Before I could dwell on this further, I was quickly sidetracked by one of the kids who sat near me. I heard a few of the other kids laughing and making loud remarks, so I turned and saw one of the kids in the class licking a glue stick. Now, I don't know what led him to do this, and I certainly won't speculate, but it was quite the site. I guess this is what first grade boys do? Either way, I got a great laugh, and it reassured me that school was going to be awesome. Even to this day, I consider that a moment of quality entertainment.

Everybody else in the class finished emptying their backpacks soon after, as Ms. Paul controlled the chaos.

"Alright class, now that we have finished unpacking, please make your way over to the rug with your show-and-tell bag," she exclaimed.

Show-and-tell bag! I screamed to myself as my stomach felt like it had just been hit with an uppercut.

Well, I guess I had finally figured out what was in everybody's bag. There was just one issue—I didn't have one. I had only brought what my mom had provided me. We had gone back-to-school shopping a few weeks prior, and I was positive that we bought everything on the list provided by the teacher.

I quickly gazed around the room and saw that everybody else had a bag with them.

Oh, no, I am going to get in trouble. Please tell me I am not the only one.

At this point, most had made their way over to the rug. I hung back. Despite my utter panic, I found a seat. To ease my emotions, I kept telling myself that nobody would notice that I didn't have a show-and-tell bag with me.

Should I just tell her? I thought as the teacher passed me on her way to the front of the rug. All the confidence I had about five minutes prior had vanished. I was nervous, scared, and unsure of what was going to happen next. I didn't know what to do except wait for my own demise.

"I brought my dinosaur" Patrick says to Anthony who doesn't look impressed.

"Hey Nick, where's your bag" Anthony asks me as he notices that I don't have anything with me.

"It's in my backpack," I lied with confidence. "I'll show you tomorrow."

"Alright now class, I will call you up to the sharing steps and give you a few minutes to show what you have brought. Please wait for your turn and give your classmate your full attention," Ms. Paul announced before Anthony could even acknowledge what I had just said.

The first day of class for almost any kid can be nerve wracking. Will I have friends? Will the teacher be nice? Where will I sit? How much homework will I be assigned?

You can double the level of anxiety felt on day one for a first grader. You want to be liked; you want to make friends; you want to appear smart. Yet, there I was flaming out, the only kid without a bag. You may as well have stuck me in a corner and put a dunce cap on my head.

I was almost to the point of shaking as I sat there cross-legged on the rug. I felt as though I had failed first grade already, without even starting. *Nobody is going to like me, and the teacher is going to be angry with me,* I worried. Ultimately, I felt left out and as if I didn't belong. All I wanted to do was run and hide.

I cringed at the thought of being called on. I had a lump in my throat and knot in my stomach. The other kids seemed excited and happy. I felt like I might puke. Negative thoughts overwhelmed me. *I need an excuse . . . I just want to go home.*

One by one, each member of the class shared what they had in their bag. Of course, we were going in alphabetical order by last name, which meant I was high on the list, but I didn't know it at the time.

"Nicholas Cidado, it's your turn!" Ms. Paul called with excitement. Not knowing what to do, I pretended like I didn't hear her.

"Nicholas, would you like to share?" she asked.

"No," I said shamefully.

"Why not?" she asked with a piercing glare.

"Because I didn't bring anything to share," I blurted. I had tucked my head down to shield myself from the embarrassment, and to avoid all eye contact. I had just told the class that I had nothing to share. Ms. Paul quickly stood and made her way over to me. She put a hand on my back to comfort me, and then told the class that I would share on a different day. I am quite sure I heard a few kids snicker as Mrs. Paul moved on to the next person without skipping a beat.

Sitting there, listening to everybody share what special items that they had brought in to show, only made me feel worse about myself. Not only did I fail to complete the assignment, but I made a scene. It was clear that Ms. Paul wasn't upset with me, so I wasn't nearly as concerned about that issue. I was experiencing the feeling of embarrassment and inadequacy, which in the moment, felt like it would be with me forever. It was the first time I felt such strong, negative emotions in my life. It felt as though the world was truly ending for me in that moment. My heart was racing, and my throat was dry. This would probably be diagnosed as an anxiety attack.

Somehow, I was able to pull it together and finish out my first day of school. I thought about how my mom could have let this happen. I was so upset, I needed somebody to blame, and I was ready to get home and let her know what had transpired.

How was I the only person in the class who didn't bring anything in for show-and-tell? The question plagued me the entire bus ride home. Of the many emotions that I was feeling, I was just disappointed that this was the first impression I would leave with my teacher and new classmates. *This is what they'll think of me.*

Once I got home, I immediately started to cry. I was able to withstand the rush of tears while at school, but as soon as I was in the comfort of my own home, the dam broke.

There wasn't even time for Mom to ask me how my first day went; the answer was running down my face.

"How could you let this happen? I was the only one in class who didn't have a show-and- tell bag to share." I was able to utter out of the hysteria.

"Well, why didn't you bring a show-and-tell bag," she responded in a very consoling, yet direct way.

"You didn't tell me I had to!" I replied.

"I can't do everything for you. You were able to get all your other school supplies together. Why couldn't you take care of this?"

As I sat there without an answer, I came to the realization that this was, in fact, my fault. Mom never beat around the bush, and she made sure that she always got her point across. Just because I was crying, didn't mean she was going to take the blame for something that I was responsible for. She saw it as a teaching moment and made sure that I would learn from it.

The truth is, I knew about the show-and-tell bag, but I had just never taken the time to put it together. All the questioning going on in my head and the pretend, confused look I wore while in class was strictly a coping mechanism. I was trying to mask the issue of me forgetting the assignment and was hoping that I could slip under the radar. But what I quickly learned was that the internal feelings of not being suited for the assignment would outweigh where I stood on anybody's radar. I had nobody else to blame but myself. I showed up at school that day unprepared.

Mom leaned in to give me a big hug and said, "Never forget the feeling you had today. From this moment on, you will prepare everything that you need, and you'll never make this mistake again. This outcome was completely avoidable."

She smiled and added, "Let's go put together the best show-and-tell bag for you to present tomorrow."

∼

How I learned about preparation

To this day, that is still one of the worst feelings I have ever experienced—the feeling of being unprepared.

At six years old, I learned the most important lesson of my life, a lesson that has resonated with me so much that I am sitting here reflecting on the experience more than twenty-five years later. A lesson that will be embedded in who I am for the rest of my life. Few people can recall much of life at age six, but for me, the experience was so deep that I could tell you every little detail of what happened on that day.

Now you may be sitting there contemplating one, or even all, of the following questions:
1. So what, you forgot your show-and-tell bag. Who cares?
2. Why does a first-grade experience resonate with you for this long? Get over it.
3. What does this have to do with preparation? Sounds like an anxiety issue at six years old.

To answer the first question, you are right. Nobody cares about the show-and-tell bag— not me, not the teacher, not my mom, not anybody in the class, and not anyone reading this book. The show-and-tell bag is meaningless, but it starts the story. You see, the bag represents a task, a performance, or a desired outcome. By forgetting the bag that day, I failed the assignment, and because of that failure, I was embarrassed and filled with anxiety, nervousness, fear, inadequacy. When you have that many feelings occurring simultaneously, I promise, you will never forget it, especially when you are exposed to it at six years old. This was one of those life-changing, childhood events that psychologists study. Often, the situations and exposures occurring during your development shape who you become later in life. To that end, I hope that I have also answered your second question. Yes, I did in fact "get over" not having a bag for show-and-tell, but I refuse to waste the lesson I learned from it. Some of our best lessons are learned in failure, not success. My failure that day left a scar of intelligence that I am forever better for.

To answer your final question, my response is quite simple; my failing that day has everything to do with preparation. I learned both the meaning and the value of preparing. But at age six, I was too young to fully grasp the concept. It has taken some time to decipher the experience and utilize the knowledge gained. This traumatic experience prodded me to improve for future endeavors. It's just like driving on bald tires in a snowstorm; you're going to skid and possibly crash. Replacing those tires beforehand helps avoid such a mishap. If you did crash, I guarantee you will replace those worn tires before next winter.

What happens when you are bench pressing heavy weight without somebody present to serve as a spotter? The weights crash down on you, and you can become seriously injured. If that happens, you'll be asking somebody to spot you next time.

And what about when somebody close to you suddenly dies? You immediately see the value in them more so than when they were still with you. That loss reveals how much you actually valued their existence. But like anything else, you don't truly find this out until after the fact.

The world has an interesting way of teaching us skills. They are often developed from failing or learned through negative occurrences. It is often these negative experiences where we have the most knowledge to gain. Because of the way I felt that day in first grade, I have made it a point to develop skills throughout my life that leave me prepared and in control of everything I encounter. It doesn't matter what the moment entails, what the task permits, or the desired outcome. I will be prepared for it.

When my mom told me to never forget the feeling, I took that quite literally and have carried it with me ever since.

Why I wrote this book

I have used preparation skills to achieve nearly everything noteworthy in my life. I am now a strength and conditioning coach at a Division 1 university. My job, simply put, is to physically and mentally prepare athletes to play their respective sport at the highest level. Everything I do is preparation based, including my approach to the development and specific training protocols I employ or advocate. Furthermore, I have been a collegiate athlete myself where my job was to prepare every day to compete on the field. I have been a student at both the undergraduate and graduate levels where my focus was to prepare for my future profession. I have had speaking engagements where I prepare a message that will resonate with my audience. I have prepared to pass exams, interviews, certifications... the list continues.

In reality, everybody is put into these same situations at various stages in life; I am certainly not a rarity. But what I have both learned and seen from others throughout my experiences is that preparation is not always viewed as a crucial step on the road to success. It is not always labeled as a priority, and I believe this is a root cause of failure and underperformance.

I am deeply interested in human behavior, and I often try to analyze and understand why people act and behave as they do. In both my personal and professional life, a reoccurring theme revolves around basic preparedness and attentiveness. It amazes me how often I have witnessed people showing up late to scheduled meetings without notice; some don't show up at all. I have always wondered how someone can show up to class without having completed an assignment, or even how one can show up to a professional meeting without having performed their own job. It baffles me to watch disorganized individuals scamper around all day getting little accomplished. I am astonished when someone tells me that they don't have time to eat lunch because they are so busy *catching up* on work. I was always confused by the same kid who showed up late to football practice every single night. And I will never quite understand the person who acts like they are the busiest person in the world and doesn't have time for anyone else.

This reoccurring theme is pervasive and worrisome. But what I have come to realize after talking to many of these harried individuals is that they have no control over their life. Everything they do is impulsive and requires zero planning. They're reactive, not proactive. They wonder why they are so tired and stressed all the time but fail to see that their life is in shambles from being disorganized. Their entire life is spent in catch-up mode, and they are continuously drained of energy. Because of this, their work, relationships, and quality of life suffer as their life spirals out of control. Many barely get by, but what they don't realize is the poor impression of people around them, and the subpar level of their performance on the job. They come to be viewed as someone who is not dependable or trustworthy. They will always have an excuse as to why they failed to operate or finish something in the manner that was expected. This population lacks the ability to prepare.

It is my belief that people who learn to prepare and stay organized encounter a lot less stress and chaos. Simple tasks become easier to execute, days become more productive, and lives become more enjoyable. But to get there, many must first realize what they are lacking and recognize those areas of their life that would improve through preparation.

If you have never thought of preparation as being a necessary or a focal point, you may still have practiced it unknowingly. After some thinking, you will realize that you do prepare in some capacity for almost everything in your life. Consider how you could improve in so many areas in your life if you work on improving and refining your preparation measures.

But before you do that, identify some areas that you personally prepare for in your own life:

- ☆ Food
- ☆ Meetings
- ☆ Tests
- ☆ Sports
- ☆ Interviews
- ☆ Presentations
- ☆ Your finances
- ☆ Your living space
- ☆ Your appearance
- ☆ Tomorrow's schedule

Even if you don't believe it yet, which you will if you keep reading, I guarantee you prepare for multiple components on this list alone, not to mention the millions of other tasks and activities you endure. The list could be extended forever, because I honestly believe that EVERYTHING you do requires some degree of preparation.

Let's start with a basic example to showcase the simplicity of the idea: Everybody must eat to survive. However, what foods you eat and how you obtain them is up to you.

Do you hunt for your food? If so, I guarantee that you spend time scoping out habitats and acquiring gearing to give you the best chance of killing prey.

Do you buy food and cook it? If so, I guarantee that you spend time preserving it to keep it fresh, flavoring it, and then adjusting quality and quantity of ingredients before cooking and consuming it.

Do you go out to eat at lunch break during the workday? If so, I guarantee that you think about where you're going to go, what time you are going to get there, what you're going to order and maybe even how much it's going to cost.

My point is that everything requires a degree of preparation, even if you do it subconsciously. Yes, I agree that there are certain instances in life that require different degrees of preparation, but on the other side of the spectrum, you will have more significant events and performances in your life where your preparation dictates the outcome. You may also find that the trivial things that require preparation matter just as much as the bigger tasks executed at an elevated level.

So, my question to you is, since you know that preparation is ingrained in almost everything that you do, why wouldn't you develop a strategy and become great at it?

My goal for this book is to first teach you the value of preparation, followed by the sharing of proven tactics that will lead you down the path of success. If you utilize the tactics in this book, you will enter every level of performance with the confidence of someone who doesn't make mistakes. And if you get particularly good at it, you may never make one. I will provide honest and simple information that you can absorb and implement into your own life. If you are alive, there will always be a necessity for you to prepare. The better you become at it, the higher the ceiling of success has to rise in your life.

PREPARE TO WIN

*How Your Approach
Dictates the Outcome*

1
Sweat More During Peace
Bleed Less During War

I COULD BARELY open my eyes. They were burning from the champagne that was being sprayed across the bar in every direction. I couldn't tell you who was standing near me while getting doused in bubbly, but I could make out blurred images of ear-to-ear smiles across everybody's face. We had just won the NCAA Lacrosse National Championship and the celebration was officially on.

The smiles, the laughs, and the stories from the celebration that day will forever be stored in my memory. To see the excitement in these young athletes after watching them accomplish a lifelong goal was a pure joy to witness. It reassured me of why I do what I do.

Amidst the chaos, I was able to briefly disengage and take a second to digest the moment. My mind instantly gravitated toward thoughts on the journey and everything that the team had been through to earn this special moment. You see, most outsiders will only see the final product. If you don't know the athletes on a personal level, it is easy to assume that they are simply just skilled and had played an outstanding game that day to ultimately get the job done and win. What you can't see from a far is every ounce of effort, moment of sacrifice, and perseverance that was endured in order achieve this outcome. We can relate this to a concept known as the *Iceberg illusion*.

When looking at an iceberg in its natural habitat, you can only see the top of it, or the portion that is protruding above the surface.

You will then assume the entire mass of the iceberg based entirely on what you are able to see. Little do you know that most of an iceberg's mass resides under the surface. The portion that is showing is often not even a third the size of the entire structure. This means that the true size of the iceberg is veiled to the onlooker's eye, which makes for a grossly underestimated assumption about the actual size. In the same fashion, for our winning team, outsiders could only see the stellar game that was played that day. What they couldn't see was the blood, sweat, and tears amassed behind the scenes when nobody was around to notice. Thus, nobody could deeply appreciate what was required to win except for those who either endured or who had been close to the process.

The journey to winning the national championship had commenced nine months prior. The team reported to campus in the beginning of September to begin both the academic year as well as the fall lacrosse season. September through December is a fourteen-week period of offseason training where the team will be both physically and mentally challenged daily. It is a crucial time of year where we build our foundation, develop our talent, and pinpoint our identity.

As the strength and conditioning coach, my responsibility is to prepare the team to have the physical capabilities to play lacrosse at the highest level. Without getting into too much detail, my main two goals are to improve athletic performance and to reduce the likelihood of injury. The program is designed to make the athletes stronger, get them faster, have them become more mobile and flexible, make them more efficient at changing direction, improving their conditioning capacity, and to make them both mentally and physically tough. If I can improve all these qualities, the coaching staff will have elite athletes who will outperform their competitive counterparts from a physical standpoint. Then, when the coaches use their knowledge and expertise to develop game plans and strategies, the team can execute at the highest level, making the program merely unstoppable. By improving these attributes, we will also become a healthier team, which enables us to operate with a full roster, or close to it. The best ability is availability, which means my job requires me to utilize a very strategic approach to gain desired adaptations to become the team we need to be. With that being said, the workouts are tailored to the game of lacrosse. I am constantly researching and analyzing the biomechanics of various parts of the game, as well as the energy system demands of each position. Without providing the detail of what they are performing during these workouts, my intent has, and always will be, to safely and efficiently challenge each of them to reach their maximum capabilities.

~

In some of my first few years as a strength and conditioning coach, I began to wonder about the importance of my role. Fully understanding that I was not the head coach of the team, or even a coach of the sport itself, I still felt as though my impact exceeded just getting athletes stronger and faster. Don't get this twisted, the sport coaches are the true leaders of the team and are responsible for any success that a team has. My role is to simply support their vision. I have also been fortunate enough to be working alongside one of the best head coaches out there, which only made my work easier. But when looking at the nature of my job, I realize that my time in developing these athletes is on an annual, year-round basis, which is different than what sport coaches do. During the offseason, I am still training them. When the sport is being played, I am still training them. This means I would be making a continuous impact for the entire year, which is more than what the athletes receive from their sport coaches. This requires strength and conditioning coaches to build strong relationships, consistently push athletes to become better, and to be there to care for and support them. I have concluded that my value is greater than what I had originally thought. The extent of my work goes far beyond that of prescribing sets and reps for a workout.

When I audited my production and what I implement on the day-to-day, I concluded that I am nothing more than a physical and mental preparation coach. I realized that these athletes are not coming to me because they want to be the fastest in the world or because they want to be the next weightlifting champion. To tell you the truth, most of them don't even like lifting weights. They come to me so I can help build qualities within them so that they are prepared to play their sport better than any competitor. I teach them to be disciplined, to be relentless, and to be fearless, which is deeply rooted from the hours of training that they endure. They go through extensive training at intensities that most wouldn't be able to sustain. They are consistent and tenacious in their approach to working on their physical abilities and the refining of their skills. They are put through grueling workouts and conditioning sessions that would make most people question even showing up. They do this because at the end of the day they want to compete and win games at the highest level. My job is to simply prepare them to do this.

Around the same time that I was auditing my role and my impact, I stumbled onto a quote that read, "Sweat more during peace, bleed less during war." The message caught my eye as I was scrolling through social media one day. After researching it, there wasn't great clarity behind the origin of the quote. Some evidence suggested that US General Norman Schwarzkopf Jr. first coined it whereas other evidence traced it to an old Chinese proverb. Regardless of the origin, the short quote had a deeply rooted meaning that I wanted to explore.

To further unpack its merit, the quotation centers around the notion that the more you prepare, the greater the ability you will have to handle adversity. To achieve success or to be more successful, you must put in the work far before the moment of conflict. By challenging yourself when things are easy, you are therefore eliminating some of the weak links in your act that can lead to either error or failure. The words promote the importance of sharpening your skills while in a controlled environment, so that when the moment comes where you have no control, you will then be ready. In short, the quote is specifically related to the art of preparation, and how we can use it to dictate the outcome in what we strive to accomplish.

Although the quote utilizes a military reference between war and peace, try to apply it to your own life by interchanging some of the words:

- ☆ Sweat is synonymous with preparation, work ethic, and commitment.
- ☆ Peace is synonymous with fortune, harmony, and control.
- ☆ Bleed is synonymous with mistake, error, and failure.
- ☆ War is synonymous with performance, competition, and challenge.

After taking some time to think about these words, and why they seemed to intensely resonate with me, I realized that this is exactly what I do as a strength and conditioning coach. My job is to prepare the athletes under controlled circumstances, so that they can prevail while under the duress of competition. Furthermore, I began to start thinking about other avenues of life where this concept is applicable. I thought of school, business, hobbies, and setting goals. I almost immediately concluded that this discipline could benefit just about anyone. I even thought about how the small tasks, such as making dinner, reading a book, or designing a spreadsheet all require a degree of preparation. I knew right away that I had to share this message and apply this principle to everything I would encounter in my own life. And in my own profession, it has since changed the way I view training and the execution of my job. When I saw the quote, I knew that I needed convey this message to the athletes I work with to get them to understand what it takes to achieve success, and for them to value the process of preparing.

∾

With the same goals in mind from a scientific standpoint that I discussed earlier in the chapter, my focus then shifted to challenging athletes beyond what they ultimately needed. It didn't make sense to only prepare them for what I knew they would be up against; I needed to get them ready for any unexpected challenge they might encounter throughout the season.

Thanks to performance technology, I have access to the exact metrics that we expect to hit in each game. This is calculated from years of research, buttressed by data from a team's previous years. For instance, I know the exact distance that each position will cover during a game, the exact number of cuts made at either end of the field, the exact work-to-rest ratio that the sport demands, a range for maximum velocities achieved, and at what points during the game they generally occur. This information is crucial for understanding the exact demands of the game, so strength and conditioning coaches like me can prepare the team accordingly. In previous seasons, I had used this data to prepare the team for exactly what they would feel and could expect over the course of a game, week, and season. This model garnered success, and I knew a lot of other programs across the country doing this as well. But after reading this quote, it changed the way that I looked at my approach. Innovative ideas began to flood my mind:

- ☆ What if in training, I challenged every area of the game just a little bit more than what I knew would be demanded of the athlete?
- ☆ What if I increased the volume of running in the offseason to more than what they would experience during the season?
- ☆ What if I incorporated more maximal velocity sprinting into training so they would become more accustomed to moving faster at greater frequencies?
- ☆ What if I manipulated the work-to-rest ratios to make the conditioning work more difficult than what would be required of them during a game?

I began to accumulate all these "what if" thoughts in my head. I then started to think about the results:

- ☆ What if the team felt fresh at the end of the game while other teams were tired because the game was less intense than what they had trained for?
- ☆ What if practices were so hard that it made the games seem easy?
- ☆ What if the team was so regimented with their treatment and body care that we never had to worry about soreness or injury?
- ☆ What if we became so disciplined that there was no room for mental mistakes on the field?
- ☆ What if we prepared this way for nine months straight and won a national championship because of it?

With all of these ideas considered, I am also very realistic; the perfect game, player, and season doesn't exist. But my thoughts coalesced around the idea that if we strive for these lofty goals, and truly prepare like we were going to achieve them, then we would surely be closer to perfection than the teams preparing for less.

September 2020 was the start of a journey that would look much different than years past. The standards had changed with just about everything we did. From a strength-and-movement standard in the weight room, to the sprinting and conditioning standards on the field, I made everything a little bit more difficult. For instance, I dropped the conditioning-test standard by two seconds, made strength standards slightly heavier compared to relative weight, and sprint time desirable ranges a bit faster. Lifts became much more difficult with increases in volume, loading parameters, and tempo. Conditioning sessions became tougher as work-to-rest ratios were manipulated to ranges that would be more difficult than they would experience in a game.

Speed and agility drills became much more competitive as we

let iron sharpen iron with the top talent in the country. Discipline became a focal point of the program. You showed up prepared to work out, or you missed out. You showed up early to practice, or you missed out. You face the same side as your teammates on all your cuts or we run more reps. You make sure all of the smaller logistical things are covered such as leaving the weight room cleaner than it was found, bringing the GPS devices to and from practice, keeping the locker room organized and touching the lines on every sprint. This was the standard or there would be consequences.

The little things mattered. It could be the difference between picking up a game winning ground ball or being a step behind because you were off on your alignment. This was all to hold them accountable and to challenge them to a greater extent. The coaching staff became relentless in enforcing these new standards.

My goal was to prepare the team for more than I knew would be demanded of them. The offseason is the perfect time to do this as we were building our identity of what kind of team we would go on to be. But at the same time, I wanted the team to know that everything they were going through was to make them prepared. Every weight they lifted, and every sprint they made put them on track to becoming an unstoppable force. By preparing the way that we did, we were gradually diminishing room for error or failure in the upcoming season.

Our outcome that year came as a direct result from the work that was put in during the offseason, just like any other year. The foundation was laid, and the elevation in standards and demand drove the team to new heights. Once we started playing, it was evident which teams put in the work and who didn't.

While other teams were beat up and injury plagued come tournament time, we had a full roster that was locked, loaded, and ready to go. We prepared that. When opposing teams would make foolish mental mistakes because they were tired, we stayed disciplined. We prepared for that. When we needed to go down the crease and score, our strength allowed us to be more physical than our opponents. We prepared that.

In the fourth quarter of the national championship game, when other midfielders were tired, our lines were just getting started. We prepared that. We prevailed because our players were better prepared.

Because of the work behind the scenes, work that gets no praise or recognition, the athletes earned the right to hold up that trophy. Outsiders may have believed that our success was purely built on talent—not something that was worked on every single day. But just like the iceberg, they would be amazed at what really took place beneath the surface.

Based on some of the ensuing conversations that I had with multiple players since the championship moment, it is clear that winners understand the process that I am trying to convey.

"Remember back in December when it was thirteen degrees at eight in the morning and you had us run a surprise conditioning test? It sucked, but the cold weather became our advantage because of it," said one player.

"Now I see why you made us do all that conditioning and lifting. Nobody could stop us," boasted another.

"Throughout the entire season, I never felt like we played anyone who was on our level. Nobody put in the work like we did," said a third.

Most may not comprehend it at the moment, but when it is all said and done, it is widely understood that preparation is integral to success. The process of working harder when you don't have to or when it doesn't seem to matter is the ultimate mindset of a winner. This is somebody who can forego the emotional attachment of doing something for immediate results, and instead believe that what they are doing now will pay off down the road.

Why was Michael Jordan so confident in taking the last shot of a close game? It's because he put his body through that same shot thousands of times in his preparation. Every time he practiced, he approached it like it was that exact moment. So, when the game was on the line, he was just doing something he had already done a thousand times prior. He built himself for that moment. You thought that one day he just randomly became the best basketball player of all time? There's that Iceberg illusion again.

Sweat More During Peace, Bleed Less During War, the name of this book, is not just a quote, it's a lifestyle and a mindset. It can be applied to every facet of life that requires any extent of either preparation or evaluation. Your approach to a certain task or area of life will be the precursor to the result that you manifest. In other words, if you push your preparation to the extreme, you will be more likely to succeed when that key moment occurs. On the contrary, if you fail to properly prepare or put in the work, you are preparing to fail. By putting yourself in difficult situations, you force yourself to grow and adapt. These certain adaptations can be used in times of need.

Preparation doesn't reward those who have not truly invested in the unseen actions that reside under surface level. But if fully committed, the results will speak for themselves. Success or being perfect may not always happen, but I can promise that you will always be closer to perfection because of this effort. There is nothing quite like walking into a life event, moment, or performance, with the confidence of somebody who can't make a mistake. Your demeanor will only be shaped by intentionally pushing the envelope within the scope of preparation. When you put in the work for an extended period, you put yourself in a position to succeed. You earn the right to be confident and to execute what you have planned and prepared to do.

Think about your life and how you can apply this quote to it. First figure out if you are taking the proper steps of preparing. And then ask yourself if you are preparing enough. Do you even know how to prepare? Do you really want the result or do you just *kind of* want it? Keep reading and you will surely find your answers.

Your approach dictates your outcome and who you want to be. If you're not willing to work harder, then you don't deserve it anyway. You must get out of your comfort zone and challenge yourself during the preparatory stages.

What most people fail to understand is that times of comfort and control do not call for complacency. Rather, it is the time to work harder. Winners, and people who are successful in what they do, use this time to challenge themselves to see what they are made of. This is where true growth occurs. You will find strength in the struggle, which will only result in later success. When adversity knocks, you now have an answer. You have prepared for this moment, maybe for even more than what is being demanded, and that is why you will succeed.

But if you want it that badly, you must be willing to prepare for more than what is expected of you.

So, start sweating.

2
Failing to Prepare is Preparing to Fail

An Aesop fable:

One by one, ants kept marching along. It was getting to be the end of the summer and fall was quickly approaching. The ant colony was finishing up their last few weeks of scavenging for food to be prepared for the long winter ahead.

The days consisted of waking up early to beat the August heat and working until sunset. The group figured that they would also be able to beat most of the competition if they started early in the day.

Initially, they would all separate and search the immediate area. Once food was found, they would signal over the rest of the family to start the hauling process back to their burrow. This process is grueling work. Though hungry while working, they understood the need to save food for the long winter ahead of them.

Every day while this occurs, the grasshopper stops by the work area in a great mood. He prances around and plays the fiddle. He asks the ants to come play with him, to which they always respectfully decline as they have work to do. The grasshopper's day consists of bathing by the pound, playing the fiddle for hours, and enjoying some time with his other grasshopper friends. He was surely enjoying the summer.

The ants enjoyed the grasshopper's music but kept working. They stayed focused and steady in their chores as they could feel winter coming. They were satisfied with their production and confident about having enough food to last them the winter. The ants could now sit back and relax knowing that they were prepared.

After only a few weeks into winter, the grasshopper stopped by the burrow. "Can I have some of your food," he asked. "I didn't have time to store up this year," he whined. "I was so busy making music, and before I knew it, summer was over."

The ants shrugged in disgust. They knew he had plenty of time but chose to allocate it elsewhere. "Making music, were you?" they cried. "Very well. Now dance!" They then turned their back to the grasshopper.

The grasshopper walked away slowly with his head down. He had no food, and it was too cold to scavenge on his own. He realized what a major mistake he made this summer.

> **Moral: If you work hard at preparing for the future, you will be in control of the outcome and won't have to rely on anybody else. The grasshopper learned the harsh reality that by failing to prepare in the summer, he was destined to fail for the winter.**

What do you think the grasshopper will do next summer?

Like I discussed, I think we learn more from our failures and negative consequences than from the positive moments. It is the fear that is instilled in us that keeps us from repeating the habits that got us there.

This will be a positive book, one that will focus on actions that you should be taking, rather than what you shouldn't be doing. But I would be remiss if I failed to mention the opportunity you gain from failing. For us to recognize necessary actions to succeed, we have to acknowledge the consequences of not doing what we should have done. We constantly learn from the trauma that we go through. It builds thicker skin and allows us to adapt and overcome. The calluses will build on our minds, our bodies, and our emotions will strengthen with every repetition of failure. Sometimes learning what not to do is the best teacher in learning what you should do.

"Failing to prepare is preparing to fail," Benjamin Franklin once said. When I see this quote, it resurrects the feeling of doubt, fear, inadequacy, and the embarrassment that I felt on that day in first grade. I relate to it, and I am sure that you can think of a time in your life when you failed to prepare as well.

It is the same feeling you endure when you show up late to an important meeting or when you wear the wrong attire to a professional event. All these instances associate a negative feeling along with them. Most of these emotions stem from what others may think of you. For me, I feared being targeted as the kid who didn't do what he was supposed to do, a class dunce of sorts.

When you are late for an important meeting, you will get judgmental stares as you walk in the room and begin your awkward apologies. Everybody says it's okay, but it really isn't. You look like a person who doesn't care about their job. Your time is more important than everybody else's in the room. You lose any sort of credibility that you had beforehand and there is now doubt creeping in about you.

Or you feel like the oddball out when you show up to an event where everyone is wearing suits and dresses, and you walk in with your jeans and polo shirt. Everyone stares at you, but nobody says anything. You know what they are thinking, leaving you with that terrible feeling of not belonging.

Each of these moments naturally affects your emotional state in a negative way. We live in a results-driven world, and as humans we can't stand to be viewed with any sort of undermining connotation. We all want to belong and feel as important as the next person. We chase success and the feeling of other people noticing. This is basic human behavior, and it is why we are so driven to succeed.

For those of you who are reading this thinking that others aren't judging you, please stop lying to yourself. If you've never been evaluated, reviewed, critiqued, criticized, condemned, commended, or judged, I truly feel bad for you. I also don't believe you. You judge others and others judge you daily. Our careers, our interests, and our lifestyles are all judgment zones.

The complement you receive about your haircut is a judgment. When you check out at the grocery store, the cashier judges what you are going home to eat. The car behind you judges your driving skills. When you give a presentation, the audience judges your appearance and delivery. The teacher assesses your work ethic because of your current grade. When you're picking weeds in the front yard, your neighbor judges your landscape aesthetics.

Perhaps the lady sitting next to you in the waiting room judges the fact that you're reading this book about preparation and scoffs at herself because she thinks she has all the answers to keeping her life in order. Next thing you know, you hear the receptionist rescheduling the lady's appointment because she forgot her paperwork. You are now judging her.

This notion of a non-judgmental environment is naïve, at best, because it is not possible. As I mentioned, it is basic human nature to judge and to be judged.

By trying to create a non-judgmental environment, you are signaling that it isn't acceptable to vocalize how you really feel about something or someone. This is more detrimental than offending somebody with the truth. If you don't know the truth, how are you supposed to change? If you're told you're great all the time, or not told anything at all because feedback isn't welcomed, how are you going to know that you actually suck? Telling someone they're lacking might hurt their feelings for a second, but it provides awareness so that person can improve. Criticism stings but it can make us stronger if embraced.

With athletes, coaches must judge talent before they make an offer to join the team. They will then judge athletic prowess and potential based upon performance every day at practice. Those deserving are rewarded with playing time. Once in the game, the athlete is evaluated based on performance again.

Within the workplace, prospective employers judge applicants before even meeting them. Based on your resume, they will decide if you are even worth interviewing. If you get the job, you are then judged based on your performance for the rest of your tenure. This includes your appearance, work ethic, commitment to the company, productivity, and so on as the circle of judgment continues.

Judgment is essential because it keeps you honest with yourself. It brings you back to reality and keeps you from the fairytale world you think you live in. But here's the thing about judgment, only one person, or maybe two or three can lie to you about your performance. They will soften the truth to avoid conflict and keep you happy. Trust me, they're not doing you any favors.

If there are a bunch of people telling you that you're fat, it may hurt your feelings but guess what, you're probably fat.

If an entire department of people at the office think you're incompetent on a subject matter. You may feel targeted, but guess what, you're probably incompetent and someone can probably do it better.

If several people tell you that your presentation delivery was poor, well guess what, it was probably much worse than they are making it seem. So, stop lying to yourself and coming up with excuses for your mistakes. Take it for what it's worth and make a change. The world isn't all sunshine and roses. Learn from your failures; then correct them. This will transform you.

Learn from the feelings you get when someone calls you fat or unattractive. If you don't want to be viewed that way prepare a plan to lose weight.

If you hate the feeling of being looked at as incompetent at work, strategize a plan to become so skilled and knowledgeable that you become a respected person in the office that others go to for guidance.

If you're feeling sorry about your terrible presentation, prepare and practice for the next time, using the feedback you received to improve your delivery.

You learn from the feeling you get when you are honestly judged. If you're a winner, and success is your goal, you will be sure to change your behavior going forward. With this information, you can then develop a plan to change.

Change begins with the process of preparation. Without it you are destined to fail again. This is why people get stuck in the same situations repeatedly. They like to play the avoidance game instead of accepting their shortcomings and striving to overcome them, which starts with preparation. You must create an actionable plan to change, and then you execute it. Failure to do this is what is plaguing the world. The notion that you can just show up and think you deserve success limits potential. Those who constantly strategize about the future and prepare for their performance moment, ultimately achieve success.

Do you think the ants are worried about the grasshopper?

3
Establish Your Preparation Tactics with Three Simple Principles

IF YOU'RE READING this book, you are most likely looking for answers. Maybe you have done some deep thinking and concluded that you are generally unprepared. Your day-to-day life is in a shambles most of the time, as a result.

Maybe you have learned through negative experiences what you need to do moving forward. That feeling of fear, inadequacy, and failure may have inspired you to change. You refuse to feel like that ever again, and the stigma associated with being unprepared makes you sick to your stomach.

Maybe you're reading this book because you make too many mistakes when the pressure is on. You can't figure out why you practice and prepare and still make mistakes. The people around you notice, and you're tired of being the person who can't perform when it counts. You thought you were doing everything you could, but the results show differently.

Maybe you are one the hardest workers out there. Everything you have accomplished has been reached through commitment and preparation. You are a high achiever who never stops trying to improve. Sharpening your preparation tactics will only make you that much more successful. You are a winner and want to keep it that way.

Maybe you're just sick and tired of losing. Throughout your life, it seems you have always been behind. You have never built strategies or committed to any sort of skill building.

Maybe you're a self-help book lover looking to add another title to the shelf because it makes you feel good inside. You love the ensuing dopamine rush from reading and inspiration.

Maybe you liked the title of the book. It sounds like something with deep meaning, and you want to find out how it could help you.

And then maybe you just don't know where to begin.

You have been on both sides of the spectrum. You have shown up unprepared, which has led to failure and all the negative connotations that comes with it. And, perhaps, you have also been the most prepared in the room leading to success at work and stoking your desire to approach every avenue of your life with that same mentality. Either way, you just don't know where to begin. You are looking to learn the tactics necessary to remain prepared for every event that you will encounter.

At the end of the book, there is a page that displays "The Tactical Plan of Preparation." It is the blueprint of all the tactics that go into preparing for success. Each tactic is governed by an overarching principle in which the messages will support. Within each principle are prescribed tactics. By mastering each principle, you set yourself up to become someone who is prepared and confident enough to take on anything confronting you. The content is progressive, and I have ordered it in this fashion by design. By setting up the book in this format, I am conveying the first order of business which is to: **Get Organized-** *Principle 1.*

This section of the book is about order. Before you can move forward, you must establish where you are going and the necessary steps it will take to get there. The tactics in this section will give you the skills to establish your desired outcome, formulate a plan to get there and stay on track.

Once you have all your ducks in a row, it is time to act. But to do this, you must first: **Become Disciplined-** *Principle 2.*

You will learn the valued skills of control and routine. These tactics will show you the ropes to staying committed and regimented. They will also show you how to avoid procrastinating and laziness. This section exposes just how badly you want to succeed. You will be forced to answer crucial questions that demand you to decide what you wish to achieve and how you get there. If you are willing to stay disciplined to succeed, the work to get there must be precise. To become fearless, flawless, and confident in your preparation, you must be in a constant quest to: **Pursue Perfection-** *Principle 3.*

Success doesn't come merely because you're organized and disciplined; you had also better be willing to put in the work to follow that pursuit. To become error-free, or to truly *bleed less during war*, you must chase perfection first. Use every skill learned from the foregoing tactics to make sure there is no room for mistake, error, or failure. You envisioned what perfection was in the first principle, now go and achieve it.

To provide the answers that you are looking for, I keep the information in this book very straightforward. Simplicity is the key to brilliance and mastery. It is my assumption that if you are never able to fully comprehend a subject matter, you will never be able to fully benefit from it. I want these tactics to be so simple that it is hard *not* to implement them into your own life. By no means is any of this information rocket science—it's commonsense science.

The ensuing chapters are designed to guide you to transform yourself into a prepared individual who is destined for success. The stories and examples I provide are all based off real experiences and encounters that I have been through, seen firsthand, or have learned from professionals in a respective field.

If you follow these tactics and incorporate them into your daily life, you will watch yourself transform into the confident person that you desire.

- ☆ You will become more organized and regimented.
- ☆ You will become committed and disciplined to achieving the task at hand.
- ☆ You will be relentless in your pursuit of perfection.

By incorporating all these qualities, your life will start to transform. Suddenly, your daily schedule becomes less about thinking and more about doing. Because of this, you can accomplish more and utilize your energy more efficiently in areas that really matter. Everything you do from here on out will behold structure. Watch with your own eyes how both your personal and professional lives excel.

Instantaneously, watch your commitment to the process of success increase. You'll take qualities like procrastination and throw it right out the window. You will learn to sacrifice what you want *now* for what you want *most*. You won't have to think about completing a task because you will have already established why it needs to be done; that's all you need. You will eliminate excuses and stay on track with proper management skills.

And finally, your standard for excellence and success will skyrocket. Because you have come this far and prepared with such integrity, every little piece of the puzzle matters to a greater extent.

It doesn't matter how big or little the task or event may be, you are just reliving the practices and principles espoused here. Production and performance will increase, and people will begin to take notice. You will be viewed in a positive light by your peers.

The return on the investment of preparation is priceless. When you are up against somebody who hasn't put in the work that you have, there is no better feeling than knowing a successful outcome is inevitable. You dictate this by your preparation. There is no more fear of failing, performance anxiety, or uncertainty of what might happen. If you have followed the principles of **getting organized**, **becoming disciplined** and **pursuing perfection**, then there are no more doubts or what ifs floating around in your brain. You make your own bed, so you decide if that's how you want to sleep from this point on.

Proper preparation produces positive outcomes. Once you've fully experienced that, there's no turning back.

GET ORGANIZED

Principle 1

4
Visualize the Moment

THE HORN ECHOED throughout the entire arena as the North Carolina State basketball team stormed the court. Head Coach Jim Valvano is seen running around the court among the chaos in pure excitement. They had just gone on an incredible run in the 1983 NCAA Men's Basketball Tournament where they would finish with a championship over highly favored Houston. It was a Cinderella story as the sixth-seeded Wolfpack ran the table and upset the top-seed Cougars.

As the party was just getting started, one by one, each player climbed up the step ladder and cut out a piece of the net from the hoop. A tradition that coincidently originated at NC State back in 1947 after the Wolfpack won the Southern Conference Championship under coach Everett Case. Each player on the 1983 team cut out a piece of the netting, turned around for a picture and cheer from the crowd, and then climbed down to help the next guy up. The process was so smooth; you would have thought they had already lived the moment.

But maybe they did.

Back in early September of 1982, before practices had begun, one of the first decisions Coach Valvano made was to tell the team that he believed they would win a national championship that year. He stressed that it would be a trying year, that they would have to fight and battle for everything that would come to them. But most importantly, he spoke about the journey they would embark on to get there, and the value of the process.

On the first day of practice, he walked into the gym with a step ladder and a pair of scissors. Looking into the faces of a group of confused young men, he signaled them over to meet him by the basket.

He placed the ladder under the hoop and then climbed up with the scissors. He cut a piece of netting off the rim, turned around to look at the team, put both fists in the air, smiling ear-to-ear, and stood there for a moment before climbing down.

Once he hit the ground, the scissors were then passed to the captain of the team. But before he let go of them for the full hand off, he looked at the group of young men and explained that to win a national championship, they would have to be prepare for every single detail along the way. They had, and in seven months they cut down that net together in celebration. So, Coach V's message was made very clear from day one; that they had better start preparing for that moment now. He then helped the next guy up, as the team watched their teammate climb up to the rim and repeat after their coach. One by one, each player went through the same motions. Indeed, when the real moment of victory came, they knew exactly what to do.

~

Creating a vision is the first step in the preparation process. If you don't know your ultimate goal or what success looks like, how are you ever supposed to arrive?

Visualizing your outcome will help you to see yourself in that position. This will then ignite the process of you working to get there. When you get your mind to picture an image of an event or area of your life that represents success, it becomes much more intimate and personal. Thus, it makes the task of getting there that much more desirable. Since you have trained your brain to recognize what you deem as success, the vision of success allows you to push closer to it. Your brain and conscious will now want to experience this vision as a whole instead of only residing as a thought. The vision makes the outcome appear more attainable. By painting a picture of perfection, you can then find out exactly what needs to be aligned to achieve it.

So, while you're sitting there, thinking about your specific idea of success, ask yourself the following questions:

- ☆ What is the end goal?
- ☆ What does it look like, sound like, smell like, feel like, taste like?
- ☆ Who will be impacted?
- ☆ Where does this take place?
- ☆ What are the emotions that come with it?
- ☆ Who is my audience?
- ☆ What will occur because of this outcome?

Typically, it is better to start off with very broad questions rather than being specific. This process captures the essence of what you are trying to achieve. The list of questions can expand forever.

By visualizing, note that the goal is to pinpoint every detail of that moment. Envision the perfect scenario where everything is in order and exactly how you would like. You will go on to spend a lot of time dedicated to preparing for this moment, so you better train your mind beforehand.

This is the catalyst tactic of the preparation blueprint. Without this crucial step, you have no direction. A big part of organization is first mapping out your plan and the steps you must take. But without a destination, you have nowhere to go.

However, visualization in itself doesn't accomplish anything. It is not a tangible action that encourages physical growth or progress. It is entirely internal and serves no purpose until further action is taken. But it remains a crucial piece of the puzzle because it provides your end point, or your intended outcome. From there you can develop your plan backward by using a method called *reverse engineering*.

Working backward, or in reverse order, removes guessing what needs to happen and in what order. By going in reverse, you have already established your desirable, finalized outcome, so now you must figure out the steps that must have occurred to get there. Here is a simple example:

Say my goal is to have all of my meals prepared for the week. I don't want to waste time in my busy schedule cooking on weeknights or spending extra money at work. I want to simply heat up my food during my lunch break and eat it. My tasks in reverse order:

- ☆ Heat up and eat my lunch at my desk.
- ☆ Grab a meal on my way out the door to work.
- ☆ Package and refrigerate all the meals.
- ☆ Cook Sunday afternoon.
- ☆ Prepare the food on Sunday morning.
- ☆ Go to the store to buy groceries on Saturday night.

When I made this goal, I was visioning myself sitting at my office desk knowing that I could just head over to the microwave and heat up my lunch. I didn't have to venture out and waste time or money buying food. I could now get more work done because my mind and body aren't worried about what I was going to eat or how I was going to get it. All I had to do was walk over a few feet to heat it up and come right back to the desk to get back to work.

Through reverse engineering, I can map out every step of my preparation to achieve the desired result. This is why visualizing the moment is so crucial. If I don't see myself eating at my desk and conserving extra time and money, maybe I would decide to be lazy and skip cooking on Sunday. But because it was a perfect scenario, it sparked my motivation to accomplish it.

The picture that you draw in your head will remain as a reference throughout the entire processes of preparation. As you get organized, and as actionable steps begin taking place, you can always resort to your visual. This is what will keep you on your path.

Before you reach success, or even embark on the journey to get there, you must first see yourself in the position. In many instances, visualization serves as a helpful tool that allows you to gauge how realistic your goal is. You can't prepare for something that isn't attainable. Well, I mean you can, but you'll be disappointed regardless of how well you are prepared.

If I sat here and tried to visualize myself designing the perfect rocket ship, I would be wasting my time. I am not skilled in engineering, aeronautics, mathematics, or anything even close to that realm. So, why would I waste my time?

So, be realistic and shift your focus to what really matters and what is attainable.

Meaningful visualizations aren't about conquering anything you set your mind to.

I hate to rain on your parade, but this isn't a book that's going to dupe you into thinking that your fairytale world is real. No, you must look in the mirror and be honest with yourself before you begin charting pursuits. Know who you are and what you think your attainable level of success is. Draw that picture in your head and start preparing for it.

This is a book about preparation, not about the *if you believe it, you can achieve it* mentality. If you need help finding out who you are, there are countless other self-help books out there that I'm sure can assist you for a while but likely will not provide you with all the answers you seek. Preparedness guidelines rely on self-awareness, which should help determine what is attainable.

The reality is that most unattainable goals are too big or ambitious. You are better off starting with a smaller goal and progressing from there. You never know, you might get to your major goal without even realizing it. Focus and preparation on small goals lay the foundation for attaining larger objects. This is known as the *size principle*. Some call it baby steps—crawling before walking before running. It rarely ends well when you skip incremental steps to focus on the larger outcome.

By achieving the smaller tasks first, you will find that it makes larger tasks much more manageable. This is not to say you can't dream big, but more so to say that you have a better chance of getting there if you build toward that goal. Dream big, but with a narrow focus on taking incremental steps. Think small scale visions first:

- ☆ The conversation with your daughter who has been struggling in school.
- ☆ Getting your first hit in baseball.
- ☆ A salary increase at your current job.

Visions can then become larger:

- ☆ Helping your daughter succeed in school and go to college.
- ☆ Becoming the clean-up hitter on your baseball team.
- ☆ Being promoted at work to a position of greater authority and compensation.

Those who prepare for and achieve success have great awareness in both the size of the vision and the reality of it occurring.

Coach Valvano believed his team would win the national championship despite being the underdog. But along the way, his focus was on winning each individual game. Yes, they had to play good teams to get to their desired outcome, but his team had battled top-tier opponents throughout the regular season, preparing them for tournament play. Just because media analysts counted them out, doesn't mean their vision of winning was unrealistic. Winning it all was a realistic goal.

NC State didn't go out on that Tuesday night in December trying to win a national championship. They went out looking to improve and take care of that required step to the ultimate vision.

Apple founder Steve Jobs had the vision of "computers for everybody" and few believed in him, initially. Others may have seen his goal as overly ambitious given his background. But it was realistic to Jobs because he had dropped out of college to allocate all his attention to working on technology and on computers for decades. Creating Apple was his vision.

Preparing requires a lot of time and effort where visualizing the moment is only the beginning of the process. It also may be the most important part of achieving goals—but you can decide that for yourself as you continue the book.

Remember, you can't get started on your journey until you know where you are going.

A fire must start with a flame.

Chapter Summary:

- ☆ Visualization is the catalyst to preparation.
- ☆ Define your perfect moment and reverse engineer your plan to get there.
- ☆ Be honest with yourself about what is realistic and attainable.
- ☆ Resort to the vision along the way.

5
Start Right Away

WHAT ARE YOU still waiting for?

You know what needs to be done and you know how to get there, so start executing.

The sooner you realize that nobody is going to do it for you, the better off you will be. Stop thinking about it and start acting on it. Your own thoughts will paralyze you, so get out of your head and take the first step.

Preparation is always your first move, in any battle. It doesn't matter how big or how small the task may be. It can be easy to remain stagnant until you develop the will to act.

Those who fail to prepare more than likely ruin their chances to succeed the second that they postpone action. If you delay the first step, you may keep deferring the process until pretty soon the moment has come and it's too late. You are unable to prepare, and now you are forced to figure it out on the fly.

I've been there before.

∽

During my English class of sophomore year in high school, it was obvious that the required workload was really starting to pick up. After some smaller projects to start the year, we were hit with our first major assignment. The assignment would require us to research a topic of our liking and put together a ten-page paper. The project had us practice processes of both the navigation of reliable sources and then the compilation and writing of our findings. We would then have to both internally and externally cite all the information to avoid any form of plagiarism, which was the main point of the assignment.

This would be the longest writing prompt in my young academic career. It was honestly quite daunting, but there was the understanding that we had two months to complete it.

Though I was initially taken back regarding the workload, I knew that I needed to prepare to build a ten-page paper. There was no way I could muster up that volume of work in one sitting. I was confident in my writing ability, and plus, I had the ability to research and write about anything I wanted, so I wasn't too concerned. Besides, anything beat writing about the outdated books that we were forced to read, or the fictional topics that put me to sleep.

Knowing how far off the due date was, I initially postponed the start of the writing process for a couple of weeks. I handled all of my immediate assignments from other classes and soon forgot about the paper. But I was quickly brought back to reality when the teacher told us to incorporate the topic of the day during class to our own papers. This was a quick poke in the brain, making me remember the work that I had been putting off. The best reminders were when she would tell us that the only homework for the given night was to work on our research papers; to me, that meant *no* homework.

I continued to procrastinate by telling myself how easy the assignment would be to complete. The only progress I had made was deciding my topic would be sports related, because that's all I really cared about. This was the vision I had for my paper.

About three weeks out from the due date, I decided that I should at least pick up the rubric and see how I would be graded. The criteria seemed to be straight forward, so I decided to open the computer and begin researching. I wrote down some good websites and articles that I thought had some useful information, finishing what would be the extent of my research for the paper. I closed my computer for the night.

The following week, life became busy. I had a couple of basketball games that would consume entire evenings after school. I had a few other projects in other classes that needed work, as well. And finally, I had a family function that weekend which would consume all my time. Before I knew it, Monday had come, and I had four days to complete the paper by the strict Friday deadline.

What do you know, Monday night I came down with strep throat. I still went to school on Tuesday because I didn't want to miss basketball practice, but after that I was exhausted and immediately needed to get some rest. Wednesday came around and I was feeling a little bit better, but not by much. My day got a whole lot worse when my English teacher reminded us that our papers were due in just two days. She advised that we make the finishing touches and final edits before submitting on Friday. I hadn't even started the paper yet.

I got home from practice that night and went straight to work, writing what I learned earlier from the scant research I had thankfully done a few weeks prior. I typed until my fingers felt like they were going to fall off before calling it quits for the night. I got a full six pages completed and thought that I had some momentum in the right direction.

When I got home from school the next night, I went straight to the computer to finish, but for the first time I experienced writers block and all a sudden had no idea of what to write. I was feeling burned out from the night before and lacked the energy to finish it off. I sat there, staring at the computer. I could barely formulate sentences. I had always heard of writer's block but had never experienced it. This is when most call it quits for the day and return to the task when rested and fresh. But since the project was due in a matter of hours, I didn't have that luxury.

It was about two in the morning when I finished the four pages that I needed to complete. I was exhausted and had no time or energy to edit or even read my paper in full. Regardless, I was just pleased that I was able to finish it off on time. I walked into class the next day and handed in my paper thinking that I had managed to pull it off.

I knew this wasn't my best work. I compressed a ten-page paper into six hours of writing with no dedicated time for editing. I figured I would get a mediocre grade but knew it wasn't refrigerator material.

The following week we received our graded papers back. The teacher pulled me aside.

"Where is your work cited page" she asked. "The purpose of this paper was to practice researching and then to both internally and externally cite all the information. You didn't do any of this. How can I give you a decent grade?"

She was a tough teacher and didn't let me redo it, despite my asking. I was so consumed with cramming it in to get it done, I had just forgotten the main point of the assignment.

As I sat there with my poor grade in hand, I asked myself why I didn't just start the paper earlier. The two days that it took to put it together were miserable, and in hindsight not even worth it according to my grade. I knew, and so did my teacher based off my previous work, that I was much more capable than what I presented.

This was a classic case of *procrastination*, a term I am sure you have heard many times and also one that has likely even consumed you at moments in your own life. Procrastination is the action of delaying or postponing something. It gives you the feeling that you can always just do it later. It creates the notion that it will all just fall in order, and that you can wing it when the time comes.

This mindset undermines long-term success. You might get by a few times or even most of the time, but eventually it will come back to get you. And even if you do *get by* or *get it done,* is it really your best work? No true success is built from subpar effort resulting from procrastination.

To provide further context, here are a few examples of this frequent problem:

You have a test coming up in your science class and you defer any type of studying or review until the morning that you have the test. You can review in the time you provided yourself, but is it enough? You managed to pull off an 82% grade, but is that really what you were going for?

Your new in-laws, who you are still trying to impress, are coming over. You desperately need to clean the house, but you keep pushing the task to the side. They will now be at the house in one hour, so you dive into the cleaning materials and get to work. You straighten up the house, set the table and vacuum. But you don't have time to clean the toilet or sink, so your in-laws will see a glimpse of your lifestyle. You did enough to hopefully impress them, that's if they don't use the bathroom.

The holidays are over, and you know you need to exercise. You're going to visit the gym but not until you watch a few more episodes of a Netflix series. You look at the clock and see the gym is closing soon so you get up and rush over there. You get there just in time to do a few minutes of cardio and weightlifting. You've barely broken a sweat and the gym closes. You technically went, but are you happy with your output?

In all these instances, you *kind of* get the result you are looking for. You *kind of* get it done. I was probably the greatest example of this with my paper. I turned it in on time and completed most of the mandatory criteria, but was it my best work? Did I get the results I strive for and want to accomplish? Absolutely not. But here is something else to think about that is notorious for hurting procrastinators:

What if there was a family emergency the night when the paper was due? I wouldn't have been able to complete it and have it turned in the next day. My teacher probably would have been nice and given me an extension, but you can't rely on those kindnesses in the real world. There are no extensions when people are depending on you, there are no extensions for the money you owe, and there are no extensions for the immediate work that needs to get done.

For anyone who thinks that my solution would have been to ask for more time to complete the assignment because I was sick or in a family emergency, you are entirely missing the point. When you are given a deadline, you prepare to complete the task at or before that given time. No excuses. In my scenario, we were given two months to complete the assignment. If it didn't get completed on time, that is entirely on me.

Had I asked for more time the teacher could have said, "I am sorry about the emergency or that you got sick, but you had two months to complete this. Were you sick the entire two months? If so, why didn't you let me know earlier?" She would have been completely right.

What if your in-laws had arrived at your house an hour early? Embarrassment, right?

What if you got a work call right before you were leaving for the gym and then had to get on the computer? Would you feel good about failing to get your workout in?

By procrastinating, you diminish valuable production time. Time where you can fine tune things. Time where you can gain feedback from others. Time that gives you the ability to go beyond what is asked of you. Time where you can prepare. Time that allows you to get more done.

There is plenty in life that you can lose and gain back, but time isn't one of them.

- ☆ You can earn back spent money.
- ☆ You can get back with your ex.
- ☆ You can crash your car and buy a new one.
- ☆ You can cut your hair too short and let it grow back.

But you can't get back time wasted.

So, what's the root of the problem? If you know what the task is or what the goal is, what is stopping you from starting?

Sometimes, it's the notion that you have all the time in the world to get it done. You believe that time won't be an issue, so you decide to wait around until you finally open your eyes at the last minute.

Sometimes, you don't care about the outcome all that much, so you wing it when the moment comes. This strategy is for the mediocre. There are many *quiet quitters* out there who walk this life with no purpose or meaning.

Sometimes, you just don't know what that first step is. You don't know where to begin and you feel extremely overwhelmed. You start getting anxiety about an approaching deadline, and it's leaving you increasingly paralyzed. Your energy is now focused on worrying instead of acting.

This problem usually arises when the task is too big or feels very demanding. Your lack of confidence puts your brain in shackles and doesn't allow you to make a move. You are more worried about the outcome than taking the first step. By creating a *negative visualization* of your result, while simultaneously making no progress, you are creating one of the worst scenarios imaginable in the world of preparation.

So, what to do? You need to start right away, which will propel you forward. By doing this, you have time to utilize all your preparation tactics. You'll be shocked to find that once you have gained momentum, you can't be stopped. You become stronger with every effort that you make. You will soon find a groove that will allow the situation to take care of itself. You will watch the nervousness leave your conscious, which will then open more mental space to utilize the energy needed to become successful.

For most, once you start something you become connected, and you behave accordingly. You now have an intimate relationship with the task and a desire to finish it. When you take a break, you will want to come back and get to work. The more time you invest into the beginning stages, the larger the return on your investment of time.

Starting doesn't require a large step; any effort forward will suffice.

As I finished high school and went on to undergraduate and graduate school, you bet I had hundreds more papers to write. To make sure I never made the mistake of procrastinating and starting when it was too late again, I decided that I would start everything right away.

When I received a writing prompt to complete, I would first

create a Word document on my computer and set the format that I would be using. I would then create the title page and save the file. Sometimes I would continue working from there. Taking these initial steps made me feel satisfied and relieved that I had already begun the process. There was no way I could get behind because I was already ahead. I soon began to realize that by just making the title page of the document, the writing process would usually take off from there. Once I was in the position to write, the words would flow.

Interestingly, I also found that when I took initial steps, I would often continue to work on the paper. I rarely shut down the computer when working on the paper, and when I did it was much easier to log back in and get back to work. You won't get this feeling until you actually begin the process.

Starting small would usually turn into finishing early. In return, this would leave me prepared for any outside influence affecting the completion of the task. It didn't matter if I got sick, was busy, or if an unexpected emergency occurred, my work had already begun which allowed me take care of other events in my life as they came up. Time is valuable, so learn to utilize it to your advantage. Here's what that could look like for you:

- ☆ Go to the gym first thing in the morning. Not much will distract you or get in the way of getting the session in at this hour.
- ☆ Wash your uniform right after the game. It will be clean and ready to go for the next game without having to scramble.
- ☆ Set aside your rent money as soon as you get paid. You don't have to worry about spending it elsewhere throughout the month.

All these actions occur right away. So, start now to give yourself the most possible time in your preparation for success.

Go!

Chapter Summary:

- ☆ Procrastination equals *kind of* results.
- ☆ There is nothing more valuable than time. Use it to your advantage.
- ☆ It's easy to get paralyzed by your own thinking. Action trumps thought.
- ☆ Small steps create momentum for large results.

6
Leave No Stone Unturned

IF YOU ARE truly striving to accomplish something, you will exhaust every possibility of preparation to get there. You will spare no effort in the journey and leave nothing to chance in the process. Every available resource will be utilized, and every option or path taken will be worn out along the way. This crucial organizational step, if completed with integrity, will leave you free of errors or mistakes, which will allow you to achieve your goals.

The idea of *leaving no stone unturned* stems from a Greek legend about a general who buried a large treasure when he was defeated in battle. As the triumphant soldiers struggled to find its whereabouts in the aftermath of the battle, those seeking the treasure consulted the Oracle of Delphi for direction. She advised them to turn over every stone on the battle ground until they found the one covering the treasure. They heeded her advice and were able to find the fortune soon after.

Before consulting with the Oracle, the men struggled in their initial search because they had no strategic plan. They aimlessly maneuvered around the battle ground, with only a hope that they would come across what they were looking for. Ultimately, they were terribly unsuccessful. Their frustration began to grow as they were not seeing any results or even getting closer. A decision was finally made by one of the leaders to seek help.

Once they received the advice from the Oracle, everything

changed. They physically lifted every stone and moved it. Every stone they moved would be left face up and would remain uncovered as the group of men swept one area at a time. By searching and moving together, they assured themselves that the entire area was covered and therefore avoided retracing their own steps. They traveled in a line to cover the battle ground in an organized fashion so that every area was thoroughly searched. Soon enough, they lifted up the stone hiding the treasure.

Initially, they were moving stones at random and putting them back in the same place. If they kept at this strategy, they could have been moving the same stones repeatedly in their search without even realizing.

The essence of this message is this: In order to properly prepare, you must be organized. Your approach needs to provide structure and guidance so there is no opportunity for anything to slip through the cracks along the way. A thorough plan leaves nothing to chance.

What plagues many people in their approach to preparation is failing to develop the plan before getting started on a task. This process requires the cognitive ability to strategically think how efficiently you can reach your goal. In most instances, this involves completing more work at the front end to achieve better results later. This tactic also requires mundane work that many people avoid. You may have to complete the same tasks repeatedly in order to reach your end goal, just like the soldiers searching for the treasure. But this part of the message corresponds to the information that you will find in the following chapters; I will elaborate more on this topic then. For now, let's drill a little deeper into the concept of leaving no stone unturned.

Here are a few hypotheticals showing how leaving a stone unturned can come back to hurt you:

- ☆ Have you ever walked into an important meeting thinking that you were fully prepared to discuss any content or handle any situation that could potentially arise? You can display your expertise on the subject at hand while your boss is firing questions at you. Suddenly, you're asked about an area that you haven't examined. You have nothing to share on the subject, but your boss needs input, now. You are then forced to explain to your boss that you lack the needed information and that you will gather it and report back as soon as possible. Because you didn't prepare yourself to walk into the meeting with answers for any potential realm of the business, your boss feels he can't depend on you.

☆ Have you ever been interviewed for a job that you desire so strongly that you have prepared yourself to the extreme? You know every detail about the position, and you provide the exact information about your strengths that the hiring panel wants to hear. The panel then asks about the company's mission, values, current operations, other departments, and specific people within the organization. You sit there dumbfounded, realizing you are not actually as prepared as you thought you were. There are two options from this point. You can either admit to the panel that you don't know the answers, or you can risk an answer or try to deflect the questions. Either way, it is not a great first impression. You didn't do your due diligence on the company and the people involved.

☆ You are trying to make a sports team, so you have been working out consistently. You know you must pass a conditioning test, so every day you go outside and practice the test in the nice sunny weather. During harsh weather you trained indoors. You have practiced so often that you feel confident about passing, despite being very close to the allotted times for each exercise.

Test day arrives and there is a torrential downpour, which drastically impacts your ability to run and cut on the field. You haven't run in the rain, so you are now forced to figure out on the fly how to sprint and cut on the wet surface while still making the standard times. During training, you chose to run indoors when the weather was bad and now you are unsure if you will be able to pass the test and make the team because of it. All that fair weather and indoor training hasn't fully prepared you.

☆ You study the course material to prepare for a multiple-choice test. You know every topic within the subject and have done many practice questions. You know the information well enough to use the process of elimination to give you the best guess. You get to class, take your seat, and are handed a short answer test. The teacher has only given multiple-choice tests in the past, and so you have never prepared for any other type of questions. Because you didn't take the time to fully comprehend the information, your short answer responses will suffer.

These are instances of failing to prepare, *fully*. Yes, you spent time preparing, but did you think about the other factors that could potentially arise? Did you exhaust every potential possibility in your plan? I can tell you that if you did, you wouldn't be telling your boss that you need more time to gather the information. You wouldn't have to dodge questions from an interview panel about the company you wish to work for. The weather wouldn't affect your conditioning-test performance. And it wouldn't matter which format questions were asked if you fully knew the material.

A prime example of not being fully prepared took place in my junior year of high school while in the middle of the football season. I am sure many athletes, even at the highest level, will relate to the following scenario:

We practiced all week in preparation for our third-round playoff game coming up on Friday night. As quarterback of a passing attack offense, I needed to spend a lot of time watching game film on the opponent's defense. Every night after practice, and admittedly during the school day on many occasions, I would watch game film.

I was trying to get a feel for which players on the other team I thought would be tougher to go up against, how I thought our receivers matched up against their defensive backs, their style of coverage, alignments, blitz schemes, and so on. The more information you can gather on the opponent, the easier it is to develop a successful game plan against them. This concept is no different than everything I have discussed in the book so far—those who properly prepare will succeed. Watching film on the opponent was a crucial piece of my weekly preparation.

On the days leading up to the game, my coach and I would discuss this information extensively. We worked together to label the opponent's strengths so we could avoid them. Inversely, we labeled the opposing team's weaknesses so we could expose them.

In all the film that we had watched, they were a team that stuck to *man principles*. This style of defense is usually successful at stopping the running game and is usually effective at rushing the passer with the different blitz schemes. It also leaves your defensive backs with little to no help in a lot of situations. These players are required to handle receivers man-to-man with no additional help.

As a successful passing offense, we were very excited to go up against this look. Most teams were forced to play a zone against us to stop our passing attack by providing more layers of coverage. But our opponent this week had never once played a zone defense, even against other passing attacks. We knew that our receivers could beat their defensive backs to get open, which made us feel confident that we could dominate by exploiting them through the air. This became our plan of attack.

Friday comes around and it is officially game day. On our first offensive possession, I break the huddle and walk to the line of scrimmage while scanning the field. I am caught off guard by what I see.

Based on the numbers in the box and alignment of defensive backs, they are not playing man-to-man defense. Instead, they are sitting in a zone, which forces me to check the play at the line of scrimmage to run the ball. If this first defensive look was any indication for how they were going to play the game, we were not prepared to proceed. We discussed how to adjust at halftime but had no Plan B to counter with.

If fully prepared, we should have been able to operate at an elevated level against the zone defense; it wasn't the first time we had ever seen it. We should have been preparing for every defense being thrown at us, not just what we saw on film. They knocked us back on our heels on the very first play by coming out in a formation that we were not at all ready for, which ended up being the difference in the game.

In professional football, coaches and players get paid to do this. They spend the entire week getting ready to compete for a single game. If they don't produce on game day, their career is in jeopardy. That is the harsh reality for high-level performers. If your livelihood depends on something, I guarantee you will prepare accordingly.

In your own life, what is it that you must exhaust to get the result that you want? To consider yourself fully prepared, what must you endure? Here are a few examples of the thought process:

An interview

Have an answer ready for any question about the position, company, or yourself. This will require a lot of research. Also, plan for how you will handle questions that have nothing to do with those three areas mentioned. You don't necessarily need concrete answers here, but you need a plan for how you will respond.

An important meeting

Find out the agenda of the meeting. Never walk into a meeting blind. Go over all relevant information about the subject and find out who will be attending. Have an idea of what could potentially be asked and how you will respond. Think about follow-up questions about past, present, or future impacts of the subject. Bring tangible material on all subject matter and have it with you for reference or even provide it for other members of the meeting.

Giving a presentation or speech

Make sure you are an expert on everything to be discussed. Have research and evidence to buttress every claim you make. Be prepared for how you will display visuals and be ready for when it isn't possible or the technology changes. How will you handle great reactions, bad reactions, or no reactions? Rehearse both the best and worse scenarios.

Developing a game plan

Prepare for anything that the other team could potentially do. Watch film and study tendencies, but also have a plan in case they totally deviate. Play devil's advocate for all scenarios when going over your own scheme to get a feel for how the opponent will react. Prepare for weather, field surface, bad calls, situation management, injuries, or anything else that could influence the result.

Hosting a party

Figure out how many people will come. Be prepared for both more than invited and fewer than invited. Have multiple food and drink options to accommodate everyone. Be able to adjust location based on weather or unforeseeable changes. Figure out where people will park and have a solution for any complaints from irritated neighbors.

In each one of these scenarios, how to prepare is obvious. But at the same time, each instance calls for planning for the unexpected. The reality is that you cannot prepare for every little factor, but what you can do is to be prepared for how you adjust when something unexpected occurs. Everybody has a plan until getting punched in the face.

For instance, let's say that you are giving a presentation to a large business group. A person in the group keeps interrupting, challenging your every word, and is being disruptive to the entire room. The spoiler appears to be drunk or on drugs. You look over at your public relations agent who then stands up and quietly escorts the man out. You don't skip a beat while this is happening.

You didn't prepare for a drunk guy being disruptive during your business strategy presentation. But what you did have in place was a public relations agent plan to handle distracting situations so that you could continue with your presentation. You essentially neutralized the drunk guy because you had a plan in place to deal with potential disruptions.

In order to be prepared and, therefore successful, plan for worst-case scenarios. Imagine what could go wrong and have a plan and people in place to cope with it. Such defensive strategies don't just come from thinking about negative or unexpected instances. This requires you to act, and to physically prepare.

- ☆ Research the company and position to the point where you know more than they do in the interview.
- ☆ Spend time developing spread sheets and combining all relative data into a presentable format before meeting with your boss to let him or her know how committed you are.
- ☆ Design and practice your presentation to the point where it would be suitable for any audience in any situation.
- ☆ Study the other opponent and all their tendencies leading up to game day so you can dictate how the game will be played.
- ☆ Review course material until it doesn't matter how they ask the question because you are sure of the answer.

When you approach your preparation with this mindset, you will be amazed by the results. You will feel organized and committed. Your confidence will radiate, and your level of performance will naturally rise as a result. When you leave nothing to chance, you are in complete control of the outcome. By exhausting all areas where you can potentially fail or be caught off guard, you are eliminating the chance of failure.

You dictate the outcome.

Chapter Summary:

- ☆ Leave nothing to chance.
- ☆ Exhaust every possibility of preparation to reach success.
- ☆ Calculate the opposition and then position yourself on the attack.
- ☆ When you can establish all threats or uncertainties, you are in control.

Get Organized is the first principle of becoming prepared because it builds the initial foundation. When your approach is organized, there is little room for mistake or error. If you master organization, you will find that the art of preparation becomes easy. On the contrary, if you are unable to organize your path to success, you open the door to failure. When errors enter the scene, in any scenario, you will start to question yourself and an overcast of doubt will soon loom.

When you combine the first three tactics of preparation, you naturally become organized. By *visualizing the moment*, you can see exactly what success looks like. When you *start right away*, the process begins by taking that first step and avoiding the plaguing factor of procrastination. And then by leaving *no stone unturned*, you make sure that you get all your ducks in a row before the real work begins.

Get organized!

BECOME DISCIPLINED

Principle 2

7
Commit to the Process

HAVE YOU EVER thought about how easy life would be if you could just wake up and accomplish your goals in an instant? We would have an infinite threshold for success by being able to think achievements into existence. There would be no level of discomfort, no obstacles to overcome, and no internal pressure of wondering if you could actually get there. Life would be easy... until the day we would become bored.

You would quickly realize that even though you were achieving success, it didn't require any skill or effort. But when accomplishment comes easy, you abruptly lose the sense of it. Although the final product is what we all strive for as humans, the true value of the moment derives from the process of getting there. This process prepares us to reach our goals no matter how short or farfetched. When you achieve success, the internal feelings of happiness stem from the roots of the journey. Arriving at your goal usually entails facing adversity, struggling with the amount of work required, or combating self-doubt. Overcoming these challenges is what makes life, and success, worth it in the end.

Committing to the process is a tactic built around consistency and resilience. As a strength and conditioning coach, I think that the weight room is a perfect display of this concept. The weight room is the ultimate evaluator of work ethic and commitment. It rewards those who consistently train for the benefit of becoming stronger, jumping higher, running faster, or becoming more conditioned. On the contrary, the weight room also exposes those who don't consistently train. It doesn't care about your feelings, how much money you make, how good looking you may be or what grades you get. All that matters is showing up and putting in the work.

This is part of the process of athletically performing at an elevated level. You must be able to show up every single day and put your body through the training. Adaptation doesn't occur by having one really good day and then taking the next three days off. You are required to impose specific demands on the body consistently to obtain the desired adaptation. This principle is intricately connected to that of super compensation and progressive overload, which both only occur under a consistent regimen.

During this process, you will feel motivated at times, and unmotivated at others, which is why I don't emphasize motivation with the athletes I train. They must become driven and be able to operate at a heightened level under any circumstance. Especially the undesirable ones. You're not going to feel motivated to work out every day. Some days you may feel tired and sluggish. On other days you may be fighting off sickness, or you didn't get a single hour of sleep because of an important exam you were studying for at the last minute (should have started right away!). These are examples of scenarios where the motivation to train is not there. But if you're driven, none of that matters. The vision of success outweighs your feelings in that moment, so you get up and get it in regardless.

When you're driven, you don't need hype-up music to motivate you to play or train well. You play well because outside factors don't affect you. If you listen to music every time you train, you will start to depend on it. What are you going to do in the fourth quarter of a football game when you are tired and there is no music to motivate you? Will you be able to perform at your best, or will you let the absence of motivation be your excuse?

What about when it's winter break and you have five weeks away from the team to train by yourself. You already got through the easy part of training from September through December because you were forced to be there, and you had your teammates and coaches to hold you accountable even when you didn't want to work out. It's freezing outside and you are by yourself, but you are supposed to be running on the field. Are you going to be disciplined and get your training in? Or are you going to let the weather influence the process?

As a coach, I have always found this concept to be funny. Athletes will ask if we are still doing our conditioning session outside because of severe weather. When winter approaches and it is below freezing in the Northeast, athletes will ask if we are canceling or still on as scheduled. My response is usually something like, "You'd consider letting the weather dictate your life?"

I usually get a dazed stare of self-realization as they process what I had just said. After all, there is not much you can say other than admitting that you would, in fact, let water coming from the sky impact the functionality of the life you live. So, they usually just stand there and accept what I had just told them on a deep level. There is nothing left for them to say, so I then explain the value of not letting outside factors affect our long-term goals. Additionally, I want them to know that we may play in nasty weather during the season, so we had better seize the opportunity to prepare for it. It's all part of the process that must be embraced.

Let me be very clear; the process is not always enjoyable while it's happening. There will be many difficulties along the way. You will be tasked with many scenarios that you don't want to do or be a part of. The feeling of defeat will eventually set in at one point or another. You may question why you have even begun and start to convince yourself that what you're doing holds no value. This is where commitment comes into play.

You must keep going. It doesn't matter how you feel; just keep moving forward. Some days you will make great progress, and others you will fall behind. You will make strong decisions some days and other times you won't be able to make up your mind. But when you commit to this process, initial outcomes don't matter. During the process, there is no time to reflect or ride the emotional rollercoaster. These tiny outcomes don't actually matter in the grand scheme. They will all be added up over the course of the entire process to eventually accumulate to your desired goal. The process requires you to focus on the systems you are using while letting the end goal come naturally as a result.

In my job, that focus is geared toward my periodization scheme, exercise selection, and training frequency among others, which are required for me to design the best program. My goal is to make all the athletes I train stronger, faster, and more conditioned. But my focus is on the systems and principles that are required to achieve this. If every principle in the program is perfect, my overarching goal will be realized.

On the contrary, if all my focus was solely based on the end goal of making them stronger, faster, and conditioned, there is no thought into the individual principles girding success. You must first focus on the process it takes to get you there, and then you need to commit to making the changes and sticking with it.

News flash. Everybody has the same goal!

Every team wants to win a championship.

Every executive wants to increase the net value of the company.

Every line cook wants to prepare the best entree.

Every real estate agent wants to sell more houses.

Every person wants to attract a significant other.

And every strength coach wants to build stronger, faster, and conditioned athletes.

Most businesses and their competitors share the same long-term goals of profitability and growth. So, why isn't everyone able to achieve their goals? Why do some businesses fail where others succeed? Simply put, it's because those who fail have not focused on the process needed to attain those goals. By solely thinking about the final product, you make yourself the same as everyone around you. Focus on your processes. Examples:

- ★ A team needs to upgrade its defensive game plan. Changing from a man-to-man defense to a zone defense will allow us it stop giving up the big play that has been hurting us all year. This is a process change with the same desired outcome of eventually winning a championship.

- ★ The marketing team needs to change how we reach our target audience. The world has changed to a digital marketplace, and the younger generation has a high demand for our products. They need to gear advertising strategies accordingly. This is a process change with a goal of improving the net worth of the company.

- ★ A manager needs to upgrade to fresh ingredients. The chefs can control portions and make sure meals taste good, but it's hard to compete with other restaurants when we are using canned sauces and frozen meats. This process change improves entree satisfaction.

- ★ You have been successful in every real estate transaction you've been involved with. However, you gain all your clients through referrals, which limits the number of houses listed with you to sell. You need to expand your portfolio, your end game. The process for doing so is to market with billboards and in local newspaper ads. This is a process change with the same desired outcome of selling more houses.

- ★ You really want a girlfriend, but you don't get any female attention when out looking to meet someone new. You get a new hairstyle, sharpen your wardrobe, and workout more at the gym. This is a process change with the desired outcome of gaining more female attention.

- ★ You need to get your athletes faster. So, you eliminate some of the longer runs and add in more resisted sprinting and acceleration starts to the program. This is a process change with the same desired outcome of getting them faster.

Achievement doesn't happen because you want it more than everybody else; it happens because of the small steps that become a focal point. When your attention is focused on the process, you may even forget the end goal, and that's completely fine because it can be distracting. Athletic seasons are long, promotions take time to get, and the product you have built isn't going to be on shelves in one week. Everything takes time, and when you are able to put your head down and commit to the tasks, without realizing it, you will arrive.

Preparation is a process, and it requires the same commitment. There is no thinking that it will just magically appear one day. You must apply yourself to get the true benefit from it. It requires constant visualization, organization, and work to achieve an elevated level of preparation. You may face moments where you feel discouraged, overwhelmed, or even have a lack of faith in what you are doing. But if you keep at it and stay committed, you will reach the level of preparedness that your ultimate goal requires.

It is not something that you can just choose to work on. Preparation is also not something that you can just partially apply and expect results. To walk into your moment prepared more than anyone else could have imagined, you must work at it consistently. It will include taking mundane, boring steps, but if you trust the process and you crave the feeling of being prepared, you will commit to getting to that level. No small obstacle will obstruct you from being in complete control of your life.

Being committed to the process is one of the most empowering actions that you can take. There is going to be a time when you step up to a challenge and you feel great going into it. You will feel driven and ready for it. Nothing will stop you, and you will achieve your goal. And then once you act you may learn that the challenge might be more demanding than you originally thought. It will be more difficult and will require more than you expected. You will start to question yourself and everything you have done up to this point. But this is where commitment steps into play. It allows you to keep going when times get tough. Commitment pushes you forward when you think things get difficult. When you feel like you can't anymore, it pushes you closer to achieving that goal. But deep down, you know everything will work out in the end. You might not know how it will happen or when it will happen. But it will. So, when you step up and you're ready to do something, *fully commit*. Commit to the process. Commit to success. Because when you do this, you can't be beaten. No barrier will stop you from what you are looking to achieve. And when you have achieved success, you will look back and be grateful for the entire process. Everything you endured throughout the journey enabled you to accomplish what you set out to do. Your success feels that much better because of the process you followed to get there.

Commit!

∼

Chapter Summary:

- ☆ Committing to the process requires consistency and resiliency.
- ☆ Everybody has the same goal. Focus on refining individual steps of the process.
- ☆ Preparation is a necessary system for success.
- ☆ Success feels better when it is earned through the journey.

8
Make it a Habit

CONTRARY TO WHAT most may believe, success does not result from a single action. Though that's what it may look like to outsiders, that moment is the outcome from compounding efforts. Many will only see the breakthrough instant and neglect to appreciate the years, days, and hours that led to it.

- ✩ The rocks you step on in the river are smooth and rounded by decades of erosion from the cascading water.
- ✩ Weight loss doesn't occur over night. It stems from months or years of dieting and exercise.
- ✩ You don't cut down a tree with a single swing of the ax. It takes striking the same spot repeatedly to eventually collapse it.
- ✩ A volcano doesn't just decide to erupt one day. The pressure in its magma base builds over centuries.
- ✩ You don't just wake up and win a championship. It is the result of practicing and evolving the game plan for years.
- ✩ Wealth isn't randomly deposited. It is the effect of compounding interest on your dollar over the course of your lifetime.

All major events or breakthrough moments start from small actions that are repeated over time. This is called *habit*. This kind of habit is nothing more than an automatic action that is performed regularly. These can be either good or bad but will shape an outcome, regardless. The habits that you perform compound, like interest, and pay off over time. In other words, we are what we continually do, a product of our actions.

- ☆ If I brush my teeth twice a day, chances are I will have rather good oral hygiene.
- ☆ If I stretch my hamstrings every day for thirty minutes, there is a strong chance I will have solid flexibility of the hamstring musculature.
- ☆ If you water your grass every day, it will most likely remain green.

We are a product of what we repeatedly do. So, if success is your end goal, create habits that become so automatic that you don't even realize you are compiling tiny steps toward a breakthrough moment. And since we know how preparation leads to success, adopting constructive habits becomes an essential tactic.

Your preparation should be a habit; your ability to prepare must become impulsive. By always preparing yourself without thought, you will naturally become a prepared person. As humans, we are a product of what we repeatedly do. Thus, if preparing becomes a habit, it becomes a part of your identity.

There is a reason why people, after losing a few pounds, go right back to their bad diets. There is a reason why people quit smoking for a month and then go right back to lighting that thing up. There is a reason why people wake up early for a week and then resort right back to sleeping their day away.

For most people, each instance involves dramatic, unsustainable lifestyle changes. However, I would argue that if you retreat from your intended habit, you may not have desired enough the result you had hoped for. When you are driven and have a sincere desire to achieve something, you will stop at nothing to get there. I realize there is a lot of research that supports physiological effects of habit forming and the struggles of escaping addiction, and I am certainly not trying to offend anybody. But the simple principle is that if you truly desire a change or if you are driven to succeed, you will shut out all excuses or impediments to get there. This is why the concept of hitting *rock bottom* before forcing change resonates with those fighting addiction. Desire alone isn't enough to initiate change if, deep down, you don't truly want it. You are getting by and are still able to operate, even with addiction. This is why people quit bad behaviors for a while and then resume.

Hitting rock bottom represents the moment in which you develop the full desire to break a habit. At this point, there is no other choice. Change or perish.

So, if you are truly driven to succeed, and you know that your preparation will be the difference maker, make your new routines or behaviors habitual. They become so ingrained in your character that they morph into a natural phenomenon. You can now devote more time to other areas of life because your routines are so automatic.

Once you can prepare for your daily lifestyle, you will find that the preparation for the actual moment or goal will become easier. You may even find that your daily preparation habits directly affect what you are preparing for.

Here are some examples of daily or weekly preparation habits that everybody should consider:

- ☆ Lay out your clothes the night before in the exact order you will put them on as you get dressed. If you put on your underwear first, make sure it is on top of the pile so you can get them first. If socks go on last, they should be at the bottom.
- ☆ Go grocery shopping and prepare all your meals for the week on Sunday night to keep in the refrigerator. Place what you are going to bring for lunch tomorrow inside of a bag the night before, and leave it next to your keys, wallet, and whatever else you take for the day.
- ☆ Fill up your gas tank on Sunday, regardless of if you need to

or not.

- ☆ When you get home from work, put a fresh water bottle inside of your car for tomorrow morning's commute and workday.
- ☆ Complete all chores on the weekend. (Laundry, mow the lawn... etc.)
- ☆ Create automatic payments for all the bills.
- ☆ Create a physical, running list that sits on the table in case anything comes up that isn't part of the normal week.

By following these daily and weekly habits, you are making life a lot easier. When your daily life becomes easier, you can put more focus, effort, and attention on your larger goals. These are all preparation style habits that allow you to operate consistently each day. These are all what I call *non-factors* in your life. When you do them repeatedly, you don't need to think about it. It becomes routine and owns zero real-estate in your mind.

For example, you will not be consumed with thoughts about what to wear while you're rushing out of the door in the morning. You have established exactly what you are going to wear and the order in which you will put it on. You can now focus your thoughts on what can help you succeed that day, in addition to getting you to work earlier.

You don't need to come home and cook dinner after a long day of work. You can utilize the time to stay later and get more done or come home and relax knowing that it is already prepared. All you need to do is simply heat it up.

You don't have to make any unnecessary stops to fill up your gas tank during the busy week. Waste no time on the computer making payments or writing checks. And don't worry about the household chores because those were completed over the weekend.

Anything that deviates from the normal schedule will immediately be written on the running list of things to do. It is now a factor that you must account for. Maybe it is a dentist appointment. It stays on the list until it's completed, freeing you from dwelling on it.

By following these habits, you are buying yourself extra time and energy. You are doing what I call *front loading* to free up space on the back end. In other words, you are taking care of foreseeable time and effort tasks now so that you have the freedom to utilize your time and effort in a more productive space later. These are tiny habits that will not lead to breakthrough moments, but they will set the foundation for which other habits will manifest.

This excess of time and energy that you acquire on the back end from front loading can now be allocated toward the work that is required to reach your ultimate goal.

- ☆ You can deposit more time into your meeting preparation with your boss.
- ☆ Spend more time writing the book that you have been trying to publish.
- ☆ Researching the company that you are interviewing for.

Being prepared for the mundane, daily structure of life will soon directly affect your ability to prepare for everything else. By making it a habit, you will find that life becomes simpler. You will eventually make your long-term goal preparation a part of your daily habits. And when you do this, you have utilized the *make it a habit* tactic to full effect.

Suddenly, you work on your book for an hour each day. No excuses, you sit down at the same time of day and put in an hour's worth of work. Pretty soon, the book will be completed. Without even knowing it, it became an automatic preparation step along the way.

Your goal for the last decade of your life has been to lose twenty pounds. You start waking up early to go to the gym before work so you can hold yourself accountable and won't have to worry about the distractions that come up later in the day that would keep you from going. In the process, your routine shows results. What you have been thinking about and half heartily working toward for the past decade becomes a reality in only a few months.

The tiny changes you make to your preparation strategy creates astonishing results. Follow these steps:

1. Recognize the need for preparation habits.
2. Make tiny changes to daily lifestyle actions.
3. Apply the same approach toward the large goal you are reaching for.
4. Make it automatic.

The steps are simple, but like anything else, the challenge is within the work. Eliminate all the excess thinking that ensues from not being prepared. Take control of all the controllables in your life. Put forth more attention to your larger goals. And then watch your preparation habits steer you toward success. Understand that your preparation allows you to succeed. But to get there, it must become a habit.

So, make it one!

Chapter Summary:

- ☆ Small actions accumulate over time to yield a breakthrough moment.
- ☆ We are what we repeatedly do. Make preparation a part of your identity.
- ☆ Use preparation habits to create non-factors. Then allocate more time and energy to success.
- ☆ Preparing must become automatic.

9
Be Willing to Sacrifice

THE ALARM SOUNDS at six in the morning. He wakes up, packs his gym bag, and fuels his body with the first meal of the day, puts on his winter jacket and hops in the car.

On this day, people will usually wake up and take some time to admire the presents under the tree. Many get dressed before heading to church. Others wake up hung over from the night before and mentally prepare for another day of celebration with family and friends. But swimmer Michael Phelps isn't interested in any of those traditions. He is headed to the pool for the first workout of the day. It's just another Tuesday. Merry Christmas.

The most decorated Olympian of all time's schedule looked something like this:

6 a.m., wake up and eat
7 a.m.-9 a.m., swim
9 a.m.-10 a.m., lift weights
10 a.m.-1 p.m., eat and nap
1 p.m.-4 p.m., daily life needs
4 p.m.-6pm, swim
6 p.m.-8p.m., eat
8 p.m.-9 p.m., spend time with family
9 p.m., bed

Phelps would eat about 12,000 calories per day. He would endure about twenty-five to thirty hours of physical training per week. He would make it a priority to obtain eight-plus hours of sleep each night. And he held this schedule for five years without missing a single aspect of this routine.

Today, he attributes much of his success to his discipline and commitment to training over an extended period. He was willing to sacrifice the freedoms of a normal lifestyle to achieve what he wanted most. Therefore, Christmas represented nothing more than just another day in his life spent becoming closer to his goals. It didn't matter if it was his mom's birthday, if a friend got sick and needed him, or if it was an important holiday. There was no compromising on his training schedule.

In the process, he lost a lot of friends because he simply did not have time for them. He couldn't have fun and make memories with the people he loved because he was so committed. He was accused of being selfish by many because he was only focused on his own success. He missed weddings, birthdays, and many other life events that he will never be able to get back. And because of this, he was widely misunderstood. But do you think he regrets any of those decisions today?

No chance.

Michael Phelps is arguably the best athlete of all time. He earned twenty-three Olympic gold medals and twenty-eight overall. To this day, even having been retired for quite some time, he still owns four world records. Through his successes, he has been able to provide both himself and his family and friends with more memories than they would have ever been able to share together had he not been such an elite swimmer. His discipline, which stems from his willingness to sacrifice, was a major driver in all that he accomplished.

∽

The reality is, many people are willing to sacrifice for what they want most, for what they want right now. In other words, the enjoyment you receive from the moment outweighs that of the end goal. Our brain plays tricks on many of us; we become complacent and take advantage of that immediate feeling. And when this happens, true progress cannot occur because the longevity of the plan is shunted by your short-term emotions.

Many are crippled by the immediate rush of emotions from being comfortable:

- ☆ Sleeping in and missing a workout because you want an extra hour of sleep, and your bed is warm.
- ☆ Eating that cupcake because you are craving something sugary, despite being on a diet to lose twenty pounds.
- ☆ Spending money on new clothes even though you need every dollar saved up for a down payment on a house.

In all these scenarios, the emotions in the moment trump the importance of the end goal. Your mind craves instant gratification as opposed to the self-control required to block it out, the collapse of self-discipline.

Riding the roller coaster of emotions usually does not end well, simply because it leaves room for complacency and contentedness in the current moment. And when this happens, you become stagnant and fail to achieve long-term growth.

What causes this confusion in the mind is the concept around wanting something versus needing something. Although it can be hard to differentiate, these two terms foster totally different approaches. Think about it, everybody has their desires:

You may want to learn a new language at some point in your life.

You want to earn a promotion at work.

You want to achieve a better marathon time.

Because these are all just *wants* in life, your mind doesn't view it as something that needs to happen. When it becomes a *need*, it registers as something much more intimate and sought out. And when this occurs, you will do more to make it happen; short-term emotions must not become a factor.

In the following examples, first see the *want* mentality by having a desire, but also having excuses as to why you can't achieve it. This is where you see excuse hijack the trajectory of achievement. Below it, see how the *need* supplies a solution that leaves no room for excuses. If it is a *need*, then there is no room for negotiation.

☆   You may want to learn a new language, but you keep putting it off because you tell yourself that you don't have the time. You are too busy working and dealing with your kids to make it happen.

☆   If learning a new language were a *need*, you would wake up earlier to devote an hour every morning to learning the language; you would sacrifice sleep to make this become a reality. Get it done before your kids wake up or before leaving for work.

☆   You want to earn a promotion at work, but you can't produce more because you have an hour-long commute every day, and you want to get to the gym and take care of other chores during the week.

☆   If getting that promotion was a *need*, you would cut the gym out of your routine for a few weeks to show your boss your commitment. You would sacrifice the temporary satisfaction derived from working for the opportunity to advance at work. Stick around the office and do extra work on the weekend to show your dedication.

☆   You want to run the marathon in under three hours. You have been stuck at the four-hour mark and can't seem to dedicate more time to running because of your busy work schedule and social life.

☆   If running a three-hour marathon was a *need*, you would skip parties on Friday and Saturday nights so you could put in more training hours on the weekend. Wake up rested, feeling better, and watch your performance improve.

☆ Making something a *need* is critical to making it become worth sacrificing for. When it just remains a *want*, you are easily lured by the instant gratification of your normal life. No change will be made, and it will take you longer to achieve your goal, if at all. You will always find an excuse as to why you can't get something done.

To further illustrate the concept of filtering out what doesn't matter and narrowing your focus, let me provide a visual:

We are in the pool when I suddenly grab your head and push it under the water. You squirm around trying to free yourself, but I do not let you up; I am in the process of drowning you. What are you thinking about in this exact moment under water? Do your lifelong goals matter? Or are you directly focused on what you are in desperate *need* of? When you are drowning, all you are worried about is getting some air. You will do anything it takes to free yourself and rise to the surface. You are not worried about a party to go to, a girl you have been chasing, how you plan to make more money, or the fact that you're a little bit hungry. The only thing you care about is getting some air. This is a *need*.

When the goal becomes a *need*, you will be unaffected by your *wants* and desires. You have no issue ignoring those to focus on what *needs* to be done. Quite frankly, your *wants* will become less relevant as you continue to narrow your focus.

∼

A few years ago, I had a desire to clean three hundred and fifteen pounds. The *clean* is a barbell movement in the weightlifting competition that requires you to move the bar from the floor to your shoulders. It is a very complex and technical maneuver. For me to achieve this goal, I had to follow a program that was designed to improve this lift. It consisted of four training days per week, comprised of heavy Olympic weightlifting and strength movements. Every day required full devotion and left my body feeling beat up afterwards.

In the first few months, I was making solid progress. I faced the normal everyday battles of training while sore, tired, and beat up. But this is what I knew I was getting into. As I got closer to the goal, it started to get more difficult to improve. This is a normal phenomenon in the strength training process and in life. Improvement isn't always linear, and you need to ride the ups and the downs of the journey. I was about twenty pounds away from my ultimate goal, but I was surely starting to plateau.

Anyone who has experience in weightlifting before can appreciate the struggle it takes to put the last few pounds on a lift. To put it in perspective, professional weightlifters train for a full calendar year to only increase by what they can hoist by five pounds. I was about twenty pounds away, which may not seem like a lot for a novice lifter, but I knew I was in for a fight to the finish.

Hurting my progress was that I had too many other goals at the same time. I was adding multiple days of conditioning on top of my weightlifting routine, as well as eating a restrictive diet. Not only was I trying to meet this clean goal, but I was unwilling to sacrifice my conditioning capacity or general physique. Eventually, I recognized what was holding me back. The conditioning was not allowing me to recover between workouts. And the restrictive diet was limiting my energy reserves, leaving me with inadequate energy to fuel my workouts.

So after about six months, I made this clean goal a *need*. I had to come to the realization that I had to sacrifice my conditioning capacity to get there. I had to sacrifice my body composition to achieve what I was setting out to do. I had set out to complete this goal in one year, and I was beginning to feel the doubt creep in. It was time to narrow my focus and ignore the outside influences. As a result, I found myself starting to make small improvements again. I was strictly committed to the program. Nothing more, nothing less.

During the next few months, I would be challenged with a few more obstacles to overcome. First, for about a month, I had nowhere to train. The weight room that I was using was getting the floor redone, so I was forced to use a makeshift training area elsewhere. These lifts also had to occur before the workday, so this would require me to wake up at 2:45 a.m. every morning. I would make my hour-long commute to campus and at 3:45 a.m. begin my training. This would take me up to about 5:15 a.m. before I would then hop in the car and drive to another area campus where I would then shower and be ready by 6 a.m. to coach my first team.

This became my norm for the next month. I had to find a way to perform at my best at 3:45 a.m. every single day. If these sessions became half-assed, I would just be wasting my time.

A few weeks later I sprained both my index fingers on a missed lift. I had a technical flaw that caused the bar to crash on to my shoulder blades with my fingers hyperextending to stabilize the weight. So, I taped them both to the respective middle finger, and trained through the pain. Every time I gripped the bar, I felt it, but I couldn't deviate from the program if I expected to hit my goal in a few months.

Various other life events popped up during this period that tried to put a wrench in my plan. For example, the July 4 holiday comes around and it's on a Monday. I have the day off from work, and my family made plans to travel to a different state to visit relatives. The only issue is that Monday is a heavy clean day, and I am not willing to miss that. So that July 4, for me was spent by myself after a morning of training while all my family and friends celebrated without me.

As you can see, there will always be obstacles along your path. It is up to you to continue moving past them, or to stop and turn around.

A few weeks later, right around the ten-month mark, I attempted my desired lift of three hundred and fifteen pounds and succeeded. My triumph didn't matter to anybody except me, and it remains a satisfying accomplishment in my life. Not because of the amount of weight I lifted; a lot of people out there can clean way more than I did.

But because of the journey and the sacrifice it took to get there. When I made the lift, my first thoughts were centered around everything that I had been through and how it was worth the sacrifices.

- ★ Waking up at 2:45 a.m. every day and sacrificing my sleep was worth it.
- ★ Training through sprained fingers and sacrificing my health was worth it.
- ★ Missing holidays and sacrificing the celebrations was worth it.
- ★ Sacrificing my conditioning capacity was worth it.
- ★ Sacrificing my body composition was worth it.

Every day was a struggle, and it required a great deal of discipline to keep at it. At times I doubted myself, and I could certainly feel the doubt from others, which is why it felt that much better to achieve. But when a goal becomes a *need*, sacrificing becomes easy. And if you don't think it is, here is a simple example that holds much more implications than a personal goal ever would:

You're sitting on the couch recovering from knee surgery. You can barely walk. Suddenly, a fire breaks out in the house and your first thought is about your child who is upstairs. I can guarantee that you will run up those stairs to get your child out of the house safely. Why? Because saving your child is more important than you being injured. Your goal is more important than the setback, so you plow through it. Protecting your child supersedes your recovery from surgery. You don't even feel the pain while running, because you are so focused on what you are doing. It's that simple.

To achieve success, you must give things up and look past what is right in front of you. I see people fail all the time because they are not willing to do what it takes to reach their goal. They are easily influenced by their current feelings.

Preparation is the ultimate form of sacrifice. To properly prepare, you must sacrifice valuable time and energy in the process.

- ☆ If you're developing a presentation for Friday, you must sacrifice every night that week to put it together. This will force you to spend less time with your kids, who want to see you. You will also miss all the big games on TV throughout the week. Every hour is important to achieving your vision, so you lock in, ignore what isn't going to get you there, and prepare the best presentation.

- ☆ If you're saving up to go on a vacation, you must sacrifice any unnecessary purchases. You won't be able to go skiing for a day, go out to dinner every night, or buy clothing just because you like it. Every disposable dollar needs to be saved up for this trip. It will be challenging, but you will learn to turn down those purchasing impulses.

- ☆ When you're preparing for an upcoming race, you must invest sufficient time and effort into all your plans. This includes your training, your diet, and your recovery. You can't go to the party on Friday when you have to train in the morning. You can't eat that cake because that sugar spike will affect your ability to fall asleep and recover. You are laser focused on performing well in the race, so you sacrifice the normality of your life.

- ☆ In your normal, routinized week, you must sacrifice your Sunday for weekly preparation. You can't take part in Sunday-Funday, go to a sports game or sit around and watch TV. Your success for the week ahead depends entirely on your ability to prepare on Sunday. You must go grocery shopping, organize your meals, fill up your gas tank, mow the lawn, do the laundry. You sacrifice one day to be successful the following six.

The highest level of success can only be achieved with the *willingness to sacrifice* tactic. If you aren't willing to suffer a little bit, ignore your emotions in the moment, and focus on the future, you are not worthy of success.

Anything that is worth striving for in life should be worth sacrificing for. The level of sacrifice is entirely up to you; just know that this will directly affect your outcome. The feeling of accomplishment and the ensuing memories will outweigh everything that you had to miss along the way. Ask any true winner in life if what they went through was worth it or not.

Victory without sacrifice has no meaning. You think Michael Phelps' mom was upset that he missed Christmas dinner?

HA!

Chapter Summary:

- ☆ Sacrificing becomes easy when your *want* becomes a *need*.
- ☆ You must be able to sacrifice what you want right now for what you want most.
- ☆ Preparation is the ultimate form of sacrifice.
- ☆ What you are willing to sacrifice to prepare, influences the level of success you achieve.

Becoming disciplined is the second principle it takes to become prepared for success for the reason that accountability is enforced on yourself. When you are disciplined in your preparation, the job gets taken care of. Nothing is left to chance, and you don't need to worry about outside factors such as emotions or excuses affecting the final product. On the contrary, if you are not disciplined, you will find every opportunity to make compromises with yourself as to why you don't need to prepare. And because of this, when it's all said and done, you will ask yourself why you couldn't fully invest.

When you combine these three preparation tactics, you will automatically become disciplined. The process is not easy, and there is never a finish line to discipline. It demands constant attention and dedication. By *committing to the process*, you grow the characteristics of being consistent and resilient to your preparation plan. When *making it a habit*, the work becomes automatic and requires little effort or real estate in your mind. And when you are *willing to sacrifice*, you don't make excuses or compromises for what needs to get done. You are unwilling to sacrifice what you want most, for what you want now.

Become Disciplined!

PURSUE PERFECTION

Principle 3

10
Be About The Dirty Work

IN EVERY FACILITY, there is a person who oversees the upkeep and cleanliness of the space. This person empties all the trash, cleans the bathrooms, and polishes the floors. They make sure the area looks presentable and is sanitary for everyone who works there or is visiting. To do this, they work late nights and early mornings. Though they are in the building every day of the week, you have never seen or met this person. So, allow me to introduce you to the custodian.

The custodian is somebody who shows up and performs undesired work every single day. You know, tasks that nobody else wants to do. Work that doesn't get recognized or valued. The behind-the-scenes job that you have no idea even happens. This operation involves some of the grossest and unsanitary labor imaginable. Work that takes grit to endure and holds no charm in its completion. They perform what is called *the dirty work*.

Some of the dirty work includes collecting the trash and bringing it to the dumpster, scrubbing toilet bowls, cleaning up spilled food and drink, wiping down mirrors, and vacuuming rugs. There is no glamour behind any of this stuff. None of these tasks require a special education or high intelligence to complete. Though undesirable, the job is essential.

Custodians don't tell you what they are going to do, they just do it. And once you realize what was done, they have already moved on to the next task.

The values of the custodian extend far beyond what you may be able to see. It's not about what they physically do, but more so the way they do it. Custodians are often prideful individuals who perform each task to perfection. They don't benefit from these services, but they recognize that everybody else certainly will.

Custodians understand that not everyone will notice their work, but that everyone will definitely notice when something is missed or forgotten. And for that reason, they are extremely diligent at perfecting their craft. People take for granted the fresh rolls of toilet paper always on the holders, the clean mirror, and the shiny floors. They don't think twice about any of these free amenities. But people notice and criticize when bathrooms, hotels, and offices are unkept and dirty.

Because they are so focused on the task at hand, custodians are unbothered by the perception of those who benefit from their work. They understand that there is no glory in what they do, and they will never be acknowledged. They are, in many ways, invisible, and by design.

So, what pushes the custodian to continue to perform at an elevated level?

- ☆ They grow powerful by operating when nobody is around to see.
- ☆ They take pride in knowing that their work is benefiting others.
- ☆ They gain strength by doing things that others refuse to do.
- ☆ They don't need the approval from anybody else because they know who they are and what they are capable of.
- ☆ They are not looking to be complimented by anybody else.
- ☆ No motivation or support is needed because they are internally driven.
- ☆ They remain inattentive to everybody around them, yet always tunnel visioned toward the task at hand.

It doesn't matter how long the job will take, how unnecessary and mundane it may be, or how gross and unsanitary it is; the job gets done.

The custodian lives to operate; they are the true masters at performing at a high level with no incentive other than the goal of execution and perfection. They take no shortcuts and the demand for their work will always be there, and so will they. The custodian lives for the *dirty work.*

The dirty work is a term used to describe the undesirable efforts put in behind the scenes that many people don't even know exist. Labor that's required, yet often overlooked. Assignments that expose the non-committed and reward the disciplined. This is a term that only successful people will be able to relate to, yet the term is frequently dismissed.

We currently live in a world based on instant gratification. People have the temptation to forego a future benefit to obtain a less rewarding but immediate prize. This concept contradicts the idea of the dirty work. Here are some examples of instant gratification:

☆ You're hungry, so you press the button and immediately get food delivered to your doorstep.

☆ You're lonely, so you text a bunch of people on your phone to start a conversation.

☆ You take the elevator instead of the stairs because you're lazy and want to get there faster.

Technology has made life easier than it has ever been before. I am not proclaiming to be anti-technology; I do think it can be beneficial in a lot of cases:

☆ You don't have to read a map or figure out where you are, just use the GPS on your phone to navigate.

☆ You don't need to hop on a plane every month to visit your grandparents. Instead, you can utilize FaceTime or Zoom to have more intimate conversations.

These innovations have transformed our lives. However, we cannot become reliant on these mechanisms because there isn't a direct transfer to other avenues of life. In other words, we cannot let these shortcuts come at the expense of work ethic. We must use them as supplemental tools and not as reliant appliances. If it becomes a crutch and we lean on it too much, we will be handicapped in other aspects of life.

These technological shortcuts teach us that we don't need to work for anything. They create the illusion that everybody and everything is there to serve us and to make our lives easier. With a click of a button, we can get what we want or get to where we are going in an instant.

On top of this, social media has glorified this instant-gratification dependence. It has created a platform where we can share how great we think we are and how interesting our lives may be. We edit self-portraits to make us look more attractive, post pictures from months or years ago to make it look like we are always traveling, and display accomplishments or successes without context. These platforms allow us to fabricate our lives and transmit an image of how we want to be seen, rather than who we are.

On social media, *the dirty work* does not exist. There are no struggles or hardships to share. It is essentially a highlight reel of one's life. Again, this is used to gain instant approval from everyone who cares to look, to feel better about oneself. It is used to show everybody only what you want them to see. If you are only showing the end product, nobody can appreciate what must have been endured to get to that point. By showing only success, many start to believe that failure doesn't exist. It has created an area where instant gratification is both desired and achievable. This is the opposite of what being about the dirty work conveys.

The dirty work is about taking every step of the process to achieve success. There are no shortcuts, and even if there are, you would never take it because there is value in the journey. It's about working behind the scenes for long periods of time to eventually reach that breakthrough moment. There is no desire for the approval of others along the way. In real life, you don't need that dopamine response of people approving your work. This isn't social media where everything is fabricated. The dirty work isn't about boasting about what you are doing or how hard you have been working. It's about doing your job without recognition or affirmation.

In meaningful areas of life, the dirty work is required, which is why this concept is getting tougher and tougher to execute as life becomes easier and easier. If you are not programmed this way and have fallen into the trap of the instant-gratification world, you will experience failure sooner than later. I truly feel sorry for the younger generations who are growing up with this mindset. They believe in the notion that they don't have to work for anything. Easy tasks have now become difficult tasks because they are afraid of the essential work. The concept of failing or doing things that they don't necessarily want to do has become foreign. For them, because of the way they have been conditioned, doing something they don't want to do is a waste of time. They lack discipline and consistency. They feel they deserve desirable outcomes without earning it. This is the ultimate form of entitlement.

Because of this, I fear that they will grow up to fail. Not because they are incompetent or lack intelligence, but because of their work ethic. I worry that the moment they sense struggle, or the moment they feel they have been working for too long without achieving success they will surrender. This is a scary thought because without the struggle or the progressing workload toward a goal, you will never experience what true accomplishment feels like. We will have a very lost and confused world if this trend continues. We will begin to lose our purpose in life as we watch matters unfold with no control over the outcome.

We will start to develop more and more people who decide to let life events become their reality instead of working to make a change. These are the groups of people who like to play the blame game. They will point the finger and come up with any possible excuse for why they failed or why their life has turned out the way that it has. This mechanism is used to lure attention away from themselves and deflect it elsewhere. They are trying to trick their own physiological state into validating their own failure by blaming others.

This generation will crumble the first time they face any sort of adversity. If your entire life you have been given handouts or haven't needed to work hard, how will you ever be prepared for failure? Despite the world we live in, true success in life is still a product of physically putting in the work and embracing the journey along the way. This is what gives human life meaning as we travel through the brief time we spend in this world.

What is even more haunting is that we have a generation who has been rewarded their entire life just for showing up. They have been given participation trophies just for trying. So maybe it is the older generations who deserve the blame for this mindset. We've given false confidence and a sense of achievement to those who haven't earned it. If you are shaped to think that you should be rewarded just because you showed up, what are you going to do when you learn that succeeding in life requires serious effort?

- ☆ You're not getting a job just because you interviewed. And you are not keeping your job just because you show up every day. You must produce.
- ☆ You're not going to win the game just because you showed up to the field with your uniform on. The team that plays better during the game will shine over their opponent.
- ☆ You're not going to find a girl to marry just because you go to social events and mingle. You must work at forming a connection and building a relationship.

Life doesn't reward you just because you show up. It requires you to work for it, even if it is monotonous and painful. If you embrace the dirty work needed to achieve your goal, you will begin to understand that just showing up isn't enough. The dirty work is entirely about your preparation. You must be willing to work. You must be willing to do what others won't.

We have already established the first two principles of getting organized and then becoming disciplined. Now it's time to add the most important part of the equation, which is the work!

Yea, it's great to have a vision because it provides direction and structure. The "If you can believe it, you can achieve it" quote is often said to help inspire growth. I would agree. You absolutely need to believe in yourself and where you plan to go. This was the basis of the first tactic. But this quote is missing the most important part of the equation—the work! Yes, you need to believe that you can accomplish success, but you better get the required work done, otherwise you don't stand a chance. Nothing will work until you do.

The dirty work is about embracing the suck. This is the concept of doing things you don't want to do now knowing that it will pay off later on. You must do today what others won't, so you can do tomorrow what others can't.

- ☆ Nobody wants to get up early, so you make sure to get up early every single day. You will now have more time to work at your craft and you will get rid of the sorry excuse of not having enough time in the day.

- ☆ Nobody wants to spoil every Sunday with household chores and food assemblance for the week. You would much rather be watching football all day, but you know you are setting up your week for success by logging in a few hours of preparation. So, you get off your ass and get it done.

- ☆ Nobody wants to be "Timmy the Typer" at the office generating all the reports for the boss. But doing so could get you that promotion you've been looking for.

- ☆ Nobody wants to sit in the room and practice delivering a presentation a hundred times. But if you do it, you will probably knock it out of the park.

- ☆ There isn't a damn person who wants to wake up on a Saturday morning and go for a run in eighteen degree weather. But you do it because you're trying to shatter your previous marathon time.

- ☆ You'd rather sleep in and enjoy Christmas day with family and friends like the rest of your peers. But your season starts in one month, so you need to gain the edge over everybody else who decided to take the day off. Your ass is in the gym.

I think you get the point.

Nobody wakes up and wants to do these things. It is an understanding of what it takes that forces you to act. The other key factor of this mindset is that nobody will see you do any of this! Nobody had to wake you up, remind you of what to do or force you to execute. It just gets done.

Your preparation is the dirty work. It's not glamorous and it doesn't guarantee you anything. It can be very mundane and repetitive at times. Most won't even know that you are doing it. The willingness to prepare is only half the battle, and I hope you have developed the plan. But if you are not willing to put in the work, you can't expect preparation to be an influential factor of your life. But I can promise you that if you perform the dirty work every day and leave your emotions out of it, your preparation will bring you closer to perfection.

You are going to be misunderstood for even trying to be perfect. Doing the dirty work consistently will leave a lot of people questioning your efforts. Accept this and move on. While everybody else is searching for that quick shortcut or solution, those who put in the work day in day out will grow stronger. When most people run away because the work looks too daunting and the end goal looks unachievable, that's when you shine. You don't hesitate or think about it; you just execute.

Nobody appreciates how prepared you are until they see the end product. You will do what needs to be done and move on to the next task. You don't require any form of feedback or recognition. If you were expecting a pat on the back, you're in it for the wrong reasons. Your investment is entirely internal, and as a result you will experience success on a deeper level. Because you are willing to put in those hours of work behind the scenes, it means that much more to you. You have grown a connection to it and that is what drives you to pursue perfection.

Do the dirty work to acquire the edge over the competition and, consequently, to eliminate error. You become fully invested in your preparation and ignore any emotional or outside factor that can influence the outcome. Be like the custodian, *be about the dirty work.*

You think the custodian was upset that he had to take care of the mess in stall two of the men's bathroom?

Doesn't matter. It is already taken care of.

Chapter Summary:

- ☆ Do what nobody else wants to. Work from behind the scenes and embrace it.
- ☆ Don't take shortcuts, look for handouts, or accept excuses. Get it done with integrity.
- ☆ Preparation is not glamorous work and doesn't guarantee success. However, it is essential.
- ☆ When you are invested in something, you have a different type of attachment to it.

11
Aim High, Miss High

HAVE YOU EVER received a piece of advice that went in one ear and then right out the other? The type of advice that you instantly doubt and therefore eliminate from your brain within seconds. Most of us think we have the superior answer, so much so that we often throw out advice before we even put it to trial. We cannot always conceptualize a simple solution for a difficult or complex task, so we tag it as void. But sometimes it may be that straightforward. And for me, I regretfully experienced this in the eighth grade.

∼

I had just endured a vast growth spurt. I went from being about 5'6" in seventh grade, to being about 6'2" by the end of the eighth grade. My athleticism was starting to take off and I fell in love with the game of basketball. However, with my new height came greater expectations. I am not talking about the standards of playing at a higher level on the court; that forecast is obvious. I'm speaking about the ability to simply dunk a basketball.

When a young boy first learns the game of basketball, he instantly grows a desire to dunk. This may stem from a father figure lifting you overhead so you can put one through the net, or from watching the greats take flight on the hardwood. Growing up watching Vince Carter, LeBron James and so many more players change the climate of an arena with a simple dunk makes it become a goal for any young basketball player. It is a magical play that anybody can admire, regardless of your interest level in the sport. You may not even be old enough to truly understand the concepts of the game, so all that really matters is seeing some rim-rattling dunks. Anybody who has ever laced the shoes up and has stepped on the court, has thought about the day that they would go on to do it.

So, with this newly developed height of mine, I began facing the pressure of achieving my first dunk. I was feeling the burden from myself, but also from the people around me. I looked at shorter guys like Nate Robinson, who was 5'9" and had already won the dunking competition multiple times while I was still struggling to get the ball over the rim.

On top of this, you start to hear the comments from friends and teammates who say things like, "If I had your height, I would be doing windmills," and "Everyone should be able to dunk at your height." My feelings weren't hurt, but I was definitely hearing the noise.

When I began to analyze the reasons for why I couldn't dunk, I wasn't able to pinpoint anything in particular. I had the height, my vertical jump was above average, and I could grip the ball with one hand. I could jump up and grab the rim, dunk a tennis ball, and touch the backboard with ease. I practiced taking off on one leg, taking off on two legs, and even taking off from multiple angles around the hoop. But every tactic usually resulted in me getting stuffed by the rim.

I was so close, yet so very far away. I was hearing the same advice repeatedly, but nothing pushed me over the hump. I was slowly starting to doubt my ability and come to terms with the fact that dunking wasn't in the cards for me.

One day in math class, some classmates and I were finished with our work and were talking about basketball. The teacher, who was a sports enthusiast, came over and joined the conversation.

"Hey, can any of you guys dunk yet," he chimed in. *Here we go again.* Now my math teacher is going to taunt me for not being able to dunk.

"Nick is almost there. He can dunk a tennis ball," my buddy says with a smirk. Also knowing that he couldn't even touch the net yet, so he had better watch his mouth.

"You're pretty tall. I figured you'd be able to get the ball down by now," the teacher replied while looking directly at me.

"If you can get the tennis ball over, you should be able to get the basketball over, too. It's not that much of a difference." he added.

At this point, I am just waiting for the bell to ring. I already sat through his boring math lecture, and *now I have to listen to this shit*, I thought.

"Next time you're going up for a dunk, I want you to aim higher than the rim. Pretend that the rim is another foot up in the air and try to dunk on that one. If you can't get there, you will still be able to dunk the ball on the actual rim on your way down. If you aim high, you will miss high," he added before walking back to his desk.

The teacher's words went in one ear and right out the other. I shrugged off his comments and went back into the conversation with my friends. I was too prideful to learn how to dunk a basketball from a math teacher.

Weeks of school passed by as the basketball season progressed and I still hadn't dunked.

There I was again, sitting in math class learning from a true perfectionist. For this teacher, anything less than 100 percent was a failure. To him, if you can get 100 percent, then you should. He taught us to be diligent and precise.

He was so extreme that you would only receive your exam back if you failed, which again, was 99 percent or less. If you received the expected 100 percent, he had already ripped it up and thrown it out. There was no reward for doing what you were supposed to. There was only fixing what was holding you back from performing at your highest level. If I learned nothing else in the eighth grade, it was to set lofty standards for myself and expect nothing for doing what I was capable of. Both great lessons.

Anyway, as he passed out our study guides for the upcoming

exam, he reminded us to "aim high, miss high." A phrase that grabbed my attention immediately because I quickly remembered that he had said it a few weeks prior.

He then explained to the class that by aiming for a 100 percent, which he thought everyone could achieve, failing is then never an option. If you strive for a 100 percent, but get two questions wrong, you end up with a 94 percent, which is still an A. Your failure is still near perfect.

For whatever reason, it resonated with me a little bit deeper hearing it a second time, and it got me thinking, *Could this actually help me dunk?*

After school that day, I went straight to the gym. I had to see if this technique worked. After warming up, I grabbed the ball and walked out to the three-point line where I would begin my build up from.

I stood there, ball in hand, and envisioned the rim being eleven feet above the ground instead of ten. I began to dribble and darted toward the hoop. I planted my foot in the ground and sprung up as high as I could. I reached the ball higher than I ever had before as I subconsciously thought about the raised rim height.

Clank. The ball bounces off the back rim and sprayed out to center court. I had missed the dunk. But this time, I wasn't upset about it; I was excited. You see, in all my failures, I had missed by hitting the front of the rim, indicating that I didn't get the ball quite high enough. Hitting the back of the rim with the ball meant that I was plenty high enough to flush one through.

I recovered the ball, retreated to the starting point, and got myself ready for a second attempt. I approached the hoop with the exact same intent and mindset.

Bang! The rim continued to rattle as I hit the ground with both feet. I had just slam dunked the basketball.

It was like a weight had been lifted off my shoulders. I was more relieved than excited, to be quite honest. A childhood goal was officially checked off the list.

The next morning, I found my math teacher right away. I wanted to thank him for his advice and talk about how changing my mindset completely changed the intent of the action. But just like a true high school teacher would, he congratulated me and then advised that I had better start using the same strategy on my math tests. I laughed and walked away. He was probably right.

∼

Aim high, miss high is a concept that is simple in theory, yet so difficult in execution. This tactic forces you to narrow your focus beyond what your original goal entails, while simultaneously setting blinders to block any form of distraction. The principle hypothesizes that if one strives for objectives that measure beyond the desired outcome, the possibility of missing the goal completely is then eliminated.

Just like that saying, "Aim for the moon, land on the stars," this tactic is centered around the idea that if you set out to accomplish just a little bit more, you will avoid an inadequate outcome. If you fall short of the target, you will at least meet your original goal. This is a physiological trick that we can play to push ourselves past our limits and ultimately achieve success easier.

This concept is widely used by snipers within the military as well as any kind of skilled marksman. However, they use the phrase "aim small, miss small" as it relates to the nature of what they do a little bit more specifically. These professionals are taught to first locate the target, then pinpoint a target within it. This becomes the location at which they aim and shoot.

By doing this, they take precision to an entirely new level. They become so fixed on the single finite point that they don't worry about connecting with the larger target. If they miss the focal point by an inch, they are still well within the target surface area. They can raise the caliber of their shot simply by aiming at a smaller target. Thus, resulting in less area for a miss to occur.

On the contrary, if the shooter doesn't focus in on a smaller point and decides to shoot blindly at the larger area, there is more likelihood of missing the target entirely. In this situation, the shooter is only trying to meet the expectation, instead of surpassing it.

Let's look at another example:

If I am jumping up on to a twenty-four-inch box, I would need to create at minimum twenty-inches worth of force to push into the ground. If I do this, I will land directly on the box with no room to spare. After a couple of jumps, I start to fatigue, and I accidently only produce twenty-three inches of force. As a result, I miss the box and fall to the ground.

If I set out to produce thirty inches of force to jump up on that same box, I will have plenty of room to spare in my landing. So, as I get tired, I can continue to try and produce thirty inches worth of force, but also have the comfort of knowing that if I don't reach that mark, I still have six inches to spare. I will make the jump every single time.

To put this tactic into further context, let's look at a few more lessons:

Golfers will use this strategy when they are putting on an uneven green. They will purposely hit the ball to a point higher than the cup's surface. By internally pretending that the cup is higher than it actually is, they leave plenty of room to miss and set up an easier next shot. Additionally, this will also allow the ball to roll back down and potentially commit, or at least get closer to the cup. On the contrary, if they missed too low, the ball would roll farther down the slope and have no chance at going in. This would also set up a challenging next shot.

Sales managers use this tactic with their teams. They purposely set ambitious sales goals to get them to perform up to standard. Subconsciously, the manager knows that the number they demand will likely not be met, and he or she doesn't actually need it to. But what this does is force the team to try and meet this threshold and therefore perform at a higher standard. When they don't reach the number, they still hit the benchmark that the manager actually needed. The manager just doesn't disclose this.

In all these instances, the goal is ultimately greater than it needs to be. This makes it very hard to execute and will set a more difficult challenge. However, this is how perfection is met. Even if the benchmark cannot be achieved, the overall goal is still obtained. For the high achievers and true perfectionists, failing to achieve a stretch goal may feel like failure, even if the overall goal is achieved. But if the bar is continuously raised, stretch goals will be met and even surpassed, satisfying even the most devout. When striving and stretching to exceed what is expected becomes ingrained, no challenge is too great.

This tactic is used by every successful individual in some capacity. It requires every ounce of focus, energy, and preparation. Because you are demanding more of yourself than you ever have before, you must prepare for it. Here are some tips to reaching this level:

- ☆ Create a strict, maybe unrealistic deadline for your weight-loss goal.
- ☆ Provide more information than your boss asked for on the reports that you are writing.
- ☆ Make a lot more food than you think you will need for the party that you are throwing.
- ☆ Put more money than you need to into your savings account after every paycheck.
- ☆ Leave your house fifteen to thirty minutes earlier for work.

These are examples of preparing for more than what is required. By doing this, you will see that your standards have risen. As a result, this will push you to improve far beyond what you thought you could achieve and leave you destined for success without even realizing it.

- ☆ You may not meet the exact deadline, but I can guarantee that you will lose weight much faster than you originally thought by simply creating this strict goal.
- ☆ The extra content on the reports may not matter to your boss

- ★ The food might still be there when the party is over, but you were prepared in case extra people showed up or your calculation was off.
- ★ You may not always get to put in extra money to your savings, but by forcing yourself to do this, you will watch that account grow faster than you originally planned.
- ★ You may arrive early at work, but by leaving this far ahead of time, you will never be late. In case there is an accident or something catastrophic occurs, you will still get there on time.

This tactic is about doing more than what is expected of yourself. It's about reaching far beyond what is required. When you learn to prepare like this, you are reducing any chance of failure. And by decreasing errors along the way, you become that much closer to achieving perfection, thus reaching success. It is a natural phenomenon that only occurs as a result of a prepared plan. If you are a true perfectionist, you may even feel like you failed by not reaching the aiming point. Though you still achieved the goal, this isn't necessarily a bad feeling. This just means that your standards have risen. You become so focused on those higher benchmarks that you forget you hit the goal along the way. When you have this mindset, you become greater than the goal itself. The standard is so high, and you have prepared this way for so long, you become perfect.

Even when you do fail, you are still perfect in the eyes of someone else. Nobody will be able to tell when you make a mistake or fall short of a goal. But to make this happen, your preparation must be perfect. Everything is calculated and executed with intent. Otherwise, this approach will hold no substance in your quest for achievement.

If you are aiming for something and you come up short, you will still be in a better place than when you started. But that isn't what this tactic is about; anybody can do that. This is about aiming for more than what is desired, and watching success automatically fall into place as a result.

Inch wide, mile deep.

Chapter Summary:

- ☆ When you aim high but fall short, you will still achieve the required outcome.
- ☆ Your standards will naturally rise as you continually demand more from yourself.
- ☆ Your preparation must be perfect in order to execute this tactic successfully.
- ☆ Eliminate the opportunity to fail by aiming high with precision and intent.

12
Get Your Mind Right

"Get your mind right!" The athletes hear me roar as they are shuffling into the facility at 6 a.m. for an offseason conditioning session. "It's time to work."

Whether it's right before a heavy set of squats, the seconds before enduring a grueling conditioning session or while they warm up before a game, "get your mind right" is one of the last things they will here me say. At this point, the athlete will now perform at the level in which they have prepared. There is no time to change and certainly no time to look backwards.

The athletes with whom I have worked with know that when I say "its time to punch in your time card" I am really trying to get their mentality right. During a game, there is no time to change who you are or what you have built of yourself. The "hay is in the barn" as I like to say. All the preparation is done and will be highlighted on the playing field.

Their level of arousal must increase as their focus locks in on the task in front of them. All their energy and thoughts should relate to getting the job done. No outside factor should influence what they are about to do. They should be confident in their preparation, and at game time, they will reap the rewards.

This is the mindset of a champion, a person who is so prepared that they overcome and surpass any obstacle that is placed before them. This person must be sharp and precise in every move that they make as they assert their dominance over the competition or task itself. While in this frame of mind, they operate off confidence, which can only come with preparation. When you play, compete, or perform knowing you are prepared, you feel like you can't lose, and you rarely will. This winning outlook stems from first being able to get your mind to this certain place.

Take a deeper look at the lion, one the most respected species in the animal kingdom:

A lion is the king of the jungle, right? But why?

Is he the biggest and strongest animal? No, that's the elephant.

Is he the fastest animal? No, that's the Cheetah.

So, what makes him the king?

His mentality.

The lion believes he is the biggest and strongest animal in the jungle so he's not worried about fighting the elephant. He believes he is the fastest animal in the jungle so he's not worried about running from the cheetah. He is ferocious and will never back down from any other animal or conflict that arises. He knows exactly what his capabilities are, and that is all he needs. His mentality is always right and for this reason, he is king.

When I was pursuing my first graduate degree, I learned a valuable lesson about mentality through public speaking. I had never been great at presenting in front of an audience, but always felt as though I should have done better. I was critical of myself and persistently searched for reasons why I would walk away feeling as though I underperformed.

One day before class, a friend and I were discussing what we would be presenting that day. He said something like, "You don't have to know what you are talking about while you are up there, but you must be able to convince the class that you do." He then added, "Most of the audience isn't actually paying attention to what you are saying. They are more interested in how you are saying it and what you look like while you speak."

As I sat there, digesting what he had just said, I concluded that he was right. When I watch others present, I am never actually paying close attention to what they are saying. Rather, it's their mannerism, tone and stage presence that intrigues and holds my interest. My friend's words completely changed the way that I look at public speaking and performing from that point on.

Think about it, have you ever listened to somebody speak or have you ever been in a conversation where you feel as though the other person has no idea what they are talking about? That's probably due in part to the speaker's poor delivery. You don't get this reaction because you are an expert on the topic either. You get it because the person sucks at delivering the content. Next time you are in one of these scenarios, try to pick up on why you are getting this feeling. This person will likely be fumbling their words around, creating awkward pauses, talking in circles, speaking too softly or loudly, and using excessive gestures.

I began working on my delivery throughout the remainder of graduate school. I also began to utilize this technique in everyday conversations.

More of my focus was put into engaging my audiences instead of wowing them with the content itself. I emphasized having a strong body posture, making direct eye contact as I spoke, making sure to speak with precision and intelligence. I also tried my best to avoid using those dreaded "filler" words that we all rely on to stall as we get a thought from our brain to our mouth. This is not to say I didn't still try to present quality and accurate information; I am just saying that my focus shifted more toward the delivery.

Based off of feedback from the professors and fellow classmates, I came off as much more confident. The audience could tell that what I was saying was well thought out, organized and intelligent. It didn't matter the context; people were listening. They would have believed anything I said, solely because of my convincing delivery. I'm not saying that this is a good thing, but I found out real fast that I could convince anybody if I actually needed to. And since I can do it, I became keenly aware of others who could talk a good game too. As they say, you can't bullshit a bullshitter.

Getting your mind right is entirely about getting to a space where you can deliver with confidence. May it be a presentation at work, a sporting event, an interview, or a sales pitch, you must radiate confident energy to achieve the success you are looking for. Get to an area where you allow yourself to be fully invested in what you are about to do. Create the mentality to perform at your highest level.

For me, this concept exemplifies what mental toughness is about. I'm sure you have either read or heard about the recent urge for everyone to become "mentally tough." If you have, you believe that through mental toughness you can conquer anything you set out to. You have probably been told to do hard things often, and to constantly push past your physical limitations. Or, you have even heard the phrase "your brain quits before the body," so you must trick it. All this to say, you are never actually learning what mental toughness is through these claims. Just because you endure difficult physical tasks, doesn't mean that you are mentally tough. Mentality is entirely different than physicality. I agree that they can both be used to sharpen each other, but you must understand what mental toughness is before you can practice the art of it. This has everything to do with the ability to *get your mind right*.

Mental toughness is the ability to take your mind someplace else. Concentrate on the goal so much that you're not distracted by external factors. When you get to this point, you can endure far more than you thought you could have. By getting your mind right, you work on your mental game. Let me give you a few examples:

- ☆ You are running a marathon, and you pull a hamstring at mile ten. Are you going to quit because of the pain? No. Focus your thoughts and energy only on the finish line, your pace, and the next step in front of you. Convince yourself that you don't have a hamstring pull. Now your mind has forgotten about the injury and only cares about the next sixteen miles.

★ You got fired from your job and currently have no income. You have two kids and a wife who depend on you to support them. What are you going to do? Whatever it takes. Start making calls, applying to every job opportunity as soon as possible. You don't sleep, you don't eat, and you definitely don't sulk. Take your mind to a place where you have already moved on. You don't think about how tired you are, how hungry you are, how sorry you feel for yourself. The only thing that matters is getting a new job.

Mental toughness is about making your discomfort irrelevant. These people that you see running ultra marathons while beat up, or the Navy Seals who practice drowning and reviving each other, excel at this concept. They compartmentalize their pain to a point where it is no longer there. The only thing they think about is the task at hand and what it will take to accomplish it. This is how winning is done.

I recognize that the concept of *getting your mind right* can be exceedingly difficult. It is easier said than done, which is why most people quit or lack mental toughness in general. There are many people who believe meditation will facilitate this process, but that's not really what this is about. Anybody can think clearly when they are at peace or relaxed. But the reality is, the only way to improve this tactic is to execute it under challenging conditions. You must force yourself to think critically while under distress. Practice taking the time to go through an internal checklist to assure that you are ready to take on the challenge.

When you began preparing for this moment or goal, you should have immediately created a vision of what the idea of success would look like. Do this again and remind yourself of the reasons you started in the first place. Look back at everything that it took to get to this point and be grateful for the opportunity you have in front of you. From here, let the information flood your mind. These should be strict, tactical thoughts on the logistics of your execution. Let the last few minutes before the moment be rich with solutions and strategies that will lead to the vision of success you have made.

News flash! You were lied to by your teachers throughout your academic career. Most make the claim that cramming in information into your brain, seconds before the exam starts, doesn't work. They may have been right if you didn't do any studying beforehand, so you were just wasting your time. However, if you prepared properly, a last-minute revision only solidifies the information and keeps it fresh.

In the moments before whatever the task may be, think about what you will say, what you will do, how you will do it, what you will feel, and so on. Be specific as these thoughts are built to keep you engaged and locked in. There is no time or room for disengagement at this point in your preparation.

Since all your physical preparation has already been taken care of, you are in the perfect position to take the time to do this. There is no running around and putting thoughts and energy into more physical preparation. You have earned the right to utilize this time for only your mind.

Picture these scenarios:

- ☆ You arrived at your interview an hour and a half early. You have already fought the traffic, found parking, freshened up your appearance, and found the building. You can now focus on what really matters—the specifics of what you will need to do to become hired for the position.

- ☆ You already have your presentation set up to the monitor in the auditorium, have put on your attire, and have made sure to take care of all other personal needs. You now have fifteen minutes to get your mind right as the audience enters the conference room. Utilize this time to engage in the material and practice your delivery one final time.

- ★ You enter the squat rack to attempt a personal record. You have already endured twelve weeks of training. Take a second to think about how you will execute. Get in the right headspace to attack the repetition with the aggression that is required.

- ★ You are warming up and getting loose for the biggest game of the year. All the practices and film sessions have been completed. Use this time to think about beating the other opponent. Build up your confidence as you visualize perfect execution in the game plan.

If you fail to utilize this final, yet critical tactic, you could be devastated by the results. You have already spent ample time preparing for this moment, which could have taken years. So why wouldn't you utilize the last day, hour, minute, second, to make sure the outcome is perfect?

The physical work is done, and the stage is set. The last step on the list is to commit mentally. If you have any doubt in your mind at this point of the preparation process, now would be the time to back out. But you have worked for too long and too hard to quit. Give your brain a chance to develop the last-second confidence it needs to take over. The mind is powerful and will gravitate toward wherever your thoughts are. You control that. Your mind follows the path you place it on.

This naturally occurs, even if it is only for a split second. This is why you must fill this portion of your preparation with only positive thinking. Avoid any distraction or negative thought. Time is too valuable at this point to be somewhere else, mentally.

- ★ Think of the tactics involved so that you go out and execute to perfection.

- ★ Think about what you have done up to this point, so you perform with confidence.

- ★ Think about success so that you achieve it.

Getting your mind right is the same thing as developing a

championship mindset. Your ability to prepare at that last second can trigger either success or failure. This process allows you to fine tune the tiny details, focus on the task at hand, build confidence and neglect any form of negativity or doubt that may creep in.

You will win. You will succeed. But you must *think it*, first. Your preparation has driven you to this point. Now embrace it, be confident and go execute. Once you gain control over your mental state and harness its power, watch your dreams become reality in the blink of an eye. The hay has been in the barn; the only missing piece is your mentality. Once you have developed this tactic, only perfection will ensue.

Get your mind right!

Oh, and by the way, the lion isn't worried about you either.

~

Chapter Summary:

- ☆ The physical preparation is complete. The last piece resides only in your head.
- ☆ Get to a place where the goal is the only focus. Pain or discomfort becomes irrelevant.
- ☆ Develop the champion mindset. A mentality where you cannot lose.
- ☆ Sharpen your mental state, harness its power, then watch yourself perform perfectly.

Pursue Perfection is the third principle it takes in becoming prepared because of the precision and focus that is required. When you are perfect in your execution, success is therefore the only dependable result. You will be able to focus on the tiny details that lead to big results. On the contrary, if you do not execute perfectly, error and doubt will soon creep in.

When you combine these three tactics of preparation together, you will become perfect as a result. Perfection is very rarely ever achieved; however, it should be constantly pursued. It demands immediate and direct actions that must be repeatable. By *being about the dirty work*, you will take pride in doing the labor that nobody else wants to do in order to achieve. When you *aim high, miss high* on a given goal, you naturally elevate your own standards and therefore reduce the likelihood of error or failure occurring. When you *get your mind right*, you develop the mindset of a champion who cannot lose. By chasing perfection, you become just that.

Pursue Perfection!

THE EXPECTED RESULT

*You Only Perform as Well
as You Have Prepared*

13
The Truth About Performance

HIGH-LEVEL PERFORMANCE is the result of diligent preparation, relentless work ethic and calculated execution. To get to this level, you must go beyond what is expected of you within each of these individual domains. This includes surpassing expectations that are set by the standards of others, as well as what is sought out intrinsically. The ability to take initiative, remain focused, and put forth consistent effort, is utterly required. As most high performers will admit, these are non-negotiable qualities that are needed to succeed at the highest level.

This elite population shares characteristics which they all access regularly. This includes punctuality, passion, integrity, accountability, to name a few. Each of these traits allows them to complete the little things, such as showing up on time, working until completion, having a positive attitude, and accepting constructive criticism. These qualities, and everyday actions, are crucial for high performers to operate on. However, these characteristics do not require any level of talent. They can all be integrated into somebody's approach by consciously acting on them. It is entirely a cognitive ability to choose and to utilize these attributes.

Anybody who has ever been successful has most likely credited their accomplishment to challenging work or other tangible traits. You hear leaders, and people of power, harp on the ability to be precise and to work tirelessly until they get the intended result. We see that people are often defined by the magnitude in which they execute these talentless traits. But the beauty in what they are saying is that it requires little skill or expertise, therefore anybody should be able to do it. Easy enough, right? *Wrong!*

If you want to be a high-level performer and wish to reach success in whatever your craft may be, all you need to do is switch your mindset. You will only need to utilize qualities and attributes that do not require talent, therefore making the act of succeeding completely controllable. Easy enough, right? *Wrong again!*

You see, the truth about performance is that those who succeed also harbor a higher degree of skill. I wish I could sit here and tell you that if you choose to immerse yourself in positivity and only put forth controllable, general actions, that you will be destined for success. If showing up early and working as hard as possible was the answer, we would have a lot more successful people walking this planet. But this is simply not the case.

I understand it is often marketed as being this easy, especially by those at the top, but it almost never unfolds in this manner. Have you ever listened to a successful, professional athlete talk about how they came to be? It usually goes something like this: "I was in the gym every day for eight hours at a minimum. I would start at three in the morning. Then I would also be the last one off the court at night. I never went to a party or put anything bad into my body. I just grinded for years and had a lot of faith in God." So, if I did all these things, I could be a successful, professional athlete as well?

What they failed to mention is that they naturally have exceptional size and overall physiques. They likely have fast-twitch muscle fibers that allow them to be more forceful and to gain lean muscle mass on their already impressive frames. They have all the genetic predispositions to be successful at their sport. These natural, talentless attributes allow this person to have a greater ceiling than their competitive counterparts. A short, slow-twitch muscle fiber guy, who has the exact same work ethic, has no chance to compete at the same level regardless of a training regimen.

Before I move on, I want to be clear about something. Genetic potential does not automatically yield success. I believe that hard work and tenacity can drive successful results in 90 percent of the cases (Yes, that's an arbitrary percentage, but you get my point). Therefore, outworking others who do not have any sort of preset skill or potential, absolutely works. But if I am up against somebody who has been given all the tools in the toolbox, while I have nothing to work with, my chance to outperform that person is significantly diminished. I am not saying it can't happen, it is just much more unlikely.

For context, there are thousands of people out there trying to make it to the NBA. They work out every day for hours and are inherently committed to becoming the best. But if you are not a certain height, have a specific body type, or have the natural athleticism required, you will be beaten out by somebody who does. Your work ethic and production will not actually pay off in most of these extreme cases.

To provide another example, let's look at the business realm. A successful salesperson is somebody who is good with people and conversation, extroverted in nature, and has a radiating degree of charisma. These are all innate traits that make someone a natural power in sales. Yes, you can improve some of these areas, and can even fake them in some situations. But they're still necessary. On the contrary, somebody who is a poor communicator and has a negative demeanor will not be as successful in sales. Each person can work on refining their skills, but the charismatic person has the advantage in this situation. They don't have to fake who they are and risk appearing unauthentic. The introvert, on the other hand, must fake exuberance, which consumes valuable energy. They're struggling with their performance instead of concentrating on the goal, which is to sell the product. Who would you rather have on your sales team, the charismatic extrovert, or the unauthentic, poor communicator?

The truth about performance is that you must have a degree of skill to succeed. Those who are pitching the idea that you must only work hard for what you desire is dead wrong as this couldn't be further from the truth. This concept only works to a certain degree before you are passed by others who have established skills. The highest level of performers are those who have the skills, but also work tirelessly at them. They can use what they have been given naturally, but also double down on all the controllable, talentless concepts that we have already discussed. This is what the best of the best, in any field, have figured out.

The top percent of performers have discovered their niche and have acted on it. They have found what traits make up who they are, what their genetic makeup gives them potential for, and then have put themselves in a position to grow. Because they are meant to do whatever they have found, they will find it extremely easy to improve. From this point on, all they must do is work as hard as possible and exemplify all the intangibles that will continue to move them forward in their craft.

Look at the late, great Kobe Bryant for example. Those who talk about him and his accomplishments talk about how hard he worked at his game. He is on record for skipping many nights out to be in the gym and had stopped at nothing to continue to improve. Kobe Bryant is somebody who found his niche, and then doubled down on it. He stood at a tall six-six with an athletically built body. He also had a father who played professional basketball who Kobe watched and learned from. He was genetically programmed to be athletic and was given all the tools to play the sport. Kobe used what he was given to drive himself to become one of the best to ever play the game. He is somebody who had both attributes going for him, which is why he became an elite member of the basketball fraternity and among the high performing population.

The good news for you is that skill can also be developed to a point where it will surpass your genetic potential. Those who are naturally gifted have an easier route to success, of course. But it doesn't mean it's the only route. There are plenty of shorter basketball players who have enjoyed much success in their basketball careers. There are also many introverts who have made a successful career in the sales world. These individuals have learned to *compensate* in order to continue to progress. The rule of compensation, however, only allows you to go so far. But it doesn't mean it can't be used to improve performance and yield success. However, you will never reach that elite performing group if you resort to a compensatory pattern during the process. In other words, you are better off finding your niche.

Finding your niche is such an important part of the preparation process. You must spend time auditing who you are and what you stand for to find your purpose in life. This is done by filtering through your strengths, weaknesses, morals, and proclivities in order to truly find the best fit for your skills and abilities. Once you discover this, you put yourself on track to becoming a high performer. You can drive your skill to the extreme and become elite at your craft.

When you are auditing yourself, be realistic about your own qualities to spare the time of putting effort into something you are not going to succeed at. If you lack in the social skills department, then maybe you should choose a profession that doesn't require you to mingle with people and be evaluated based on your presence. Find a computer-based job where you can operate by yourself. If you have terrible body coordination, you should look at other avenues outside the realm of sports and movement. Learn to sit in a chair and play an instrument. If you are strong with numbers and equations, you should look into a career that require you to make calculations and force you to think critically. Go to engineering school to sharpen your mind further.

This process requires an honest and diligent evaluation of yourself. But when done correctly, you will target an area that you are destined to succeed in. When your niche is identified, the real work can begin. This is when the pursuit of perfection within your preparation will commence. You will then learn to build on what you already possess.

On the complete other side of the spectrum, I want to bring light to those who waste natural talent and touch on the effects that it has on their performance. Those who embody a certain set of skills, yet fail to put it to work, will soon lose the benefit of it. If you are talented in a particular trade and you don't exercise the ability, you risk mediocrity. Without a work ethic and the qualities that allow you to grow, your natural abilities become dormant. This then provides room for those who don't have your natural ability to work tirelessly, catch up, and even surpass you. It's like the quote, "Hard work beats talent, when talent fails to work hard." When talent decides that they don't have to work, they soon become a low performer who just so happens to have a skill.

In general, most low performers have this illusion of *choice* ingrained in their brains. This is something that a high performer has excluded from their vocabulary and life. Simply put, it's the mentality that individuals can do whatever they please and still expect desirable results. In their brains, he or she develops the illusion that they have all these choices and options for what needs to be done to succeed. But the fact is that if you really want to be good, to be great, to be a high performer, you don't have the luxury of picking and choosing. It takes what it takes to achieve success. You must execute what needs to be executed to get there. There is no alternative or easier route to reaching this point. As soon as you start making choices, you lose the right to expect success.

Look at all the weekend warriors on the golf course, for example. They will go out and play a round on the weekend, shoot a terrible score and then become frustrated with the results. They may even pull a Happy Gilmore and start throwing their clubs and begin to break all course etiquette. Well, what are you mad at? Did you really expect to play well? They play a highly technical sport that takes years and years to master. If you watch professional golfers, athletes who practice and play all day, every day for years on end, even they have bad days. So, what gives you the right to get angry at your performance when you play one of the most challenging games once a week or less? These people haven't earned the right to get angry. They don't have enough sweat equity in the game.

How are you going to be mad at yourself for butchering a presentation? You didn't practice or review any of the material. Of course, you are going to get up there and look uneducated.

You really expected to land the job when you couldn't even provide relevant information drawn from any of your previous experiences? How would they feel comfortable hiring you for that position?

The notion that you can just show up and succeed needs to be eliminated from everybody's psyche.

What is also plaguing our world right now is the self-development space. Everybody is more interested in the next best shortcut or coolest new practice to promote self- care and development. While I think this area is important in everyone's life, the reality is, just like everything else, these short-term solutions do not yield long-term results. And in some cases, any results at all. There is less focus on what really matters in production and performance, and more emphasis on creating a hack.

Many of these self-help books, publications, or videos promote taking cold showers, meditating, waking up and reading your affirmations in the mirror, and so on and so forth. If you want to do these things, great, but understand that this is not self-development. These modalities are used to help you get to a place where you can better function in the day-to-day grind. These are not substitutions or tricks that lead to instant success in themselves. I can guarantee that the person who is doing cold showers twice a day, mediating for an hour, reading affirmations in the mirror, and taking a sauna is not accomplishing nearly as much as the guy who has a one task list written out every day, and a pen to cross off when an item is complete. This guy isn't interested in short cuts or instant gratification. If it's on the list, it gets done. No questions. No excuses. While the other guy is busy meditating, he's actually getting work done.

My point behind this message is that performance is entirely related to work production. It simply comes down to the notion that there are no choices or substitutes, only the work that must get done. You can't sugar coat the reality of the expected result and hope for the best. Internally, you understand what it takes to get there, and you can't let anything pull you off track.

If you are skilled in a certain area, you better be willing to work because you're going to need every repetition you can get in order to compete with those who have natural ability. Likewise, if you have found your niche, you better be up and at it every day trying to outwork those who lack skill because they're doing all they can to out compete you. Just like the story of the lion and the gazelle:

> **Every morning a gazelle wakes up and understands that it must outrun the fastest lion, or it will be killed. Every morning, a lion wakes up and understands that it must run faster than the slowest gazelle, or it will starve to death. So, it doesn't matter if you are the lion or the gazelle, when the sun comes up, you'd better be running.**

If you aren't putting in the work to prepare for the moment, don't be surprised when you fail miserably. On the contrary, if you are putting in the required work every single day, don't be surprised when you eventually succeed. Before the moment has even come, you will have already known the outcome. If you decided to take days off along the way, show up late a few times, leave things up to chance, it will show in your execution. So, before you enter the situation, don't try to hope that it will go as you desire. You should have been making that desire a reality during your preparation. If you utilize all the preparation tactics, your performance will present itself accordingly. Even if you try to trick yourself and pretend like it should go a certain way, deep down you know what type of sweat equity you have invested, therefore you will have to live with the result. Whether good or bad, it was manifested by your actions. Your ability to utilize your skills, along with the intangibles will give you the expected result.

It comes down to how much you are willing to prepare.

And that's the truth.

14
Self-Defeat is Your Own Dispute

When the dust finally settles, you are responsible for the outcome. In a results-driven world, it is widely understood that you must produce to survive. Nobody is interested in your excuses, what you have done in the past, or what you plan to do in the future. Employers, coaches, leaders, and others who are high up the chain of command are strictly interested in what you can do *now*.

Unless you are at the very top, somebody is appraising your value. You will be evaluated on every aspect of your operation from an efficiency standpoint, and then on what you are able to present. Those who display proficiency in these areas will be rewarded accordingly.

- ☆ The pitcher who leads the league in ERA (earned run average) will sign a new contract at the end of the season guaranteeing him more money and job security.
- ☆ The real estate agent who sells the most houses will receive a bonus at the end of the year to reward the value she has added to the agency.
- ☆ The intern who displays high intelligence, a strong work ethic, and commitment to the company will then be promoted into a full-time position

Simply put, arduous work pays off. It is surely everyone's goal to be recognized and acknowledged for their work in hopes of receiving some kind of reward. This also serves as an incentive to perform at an elevated level. However, there is a reason why every pitcher isn't on a maximum pay contract. There is a reason why only one real estate agent receives bonus money at the end of the year. There is a reason why only one intern from the batch gets promoted to a full-time position. Success is hard to come by and not everybody fits the suit. Not everybody is willing to relentlessly prepare to put themselves in a fighting position. Not everyone is committed to the company or the organization. And therefore, not everybody is able to constantly produce and advance. And, just like how there are rewards for the top producers, there are also consequences for the underperformers.

- ☆ The pitcher who is getting shelled by the league and hoists up their ERA to well above the league average will not get signed again and may even be traded or demoted to the minor leagues. They will make significantly less money and will lose many professional privileges.
- ☆ The real estate agent who underperforms will be given less assistance by the agency in terms of marketing, market leads, clients to work with and growth opportunities. Their income and production will then suffer even more.
- ☆ The intern who doesn't display commitment to the company, or any type of useful intelligence or work ethic, will be slighted with a kick out the door upon completion. They will not have earned a job and will suffer when trying to get the company to recommend them for a position elsewhere.

This is a results-driven world where your skills must be constantly sharpened and evolved to meet the needs of production. But the good news is that the outcome is controlled by you and your ability to prepare. Your preparation allows you to operate at an elevated level. Your ability to stay organized keeps you on top of your tasks. Nothing will slip through the cracks, and you will accomplish everything that you need to do in your position. Becoming disciplined will force you to work through adversity. It will allow you to keep producing even as monotony and mediocrity fill the air around you. And finally, the pursuit of perfection will keep you among the elite. Others, who follow the same mentality that you do, may be able to keep up with you, but will never surpass you if the push remains there.

All this to say, you control your own destiny. Once you have developed or have earned a position, it is already known that you have what it takes to produce.

- ☆ A major league pitcher is still phenomenal at what he does, regardless of what happens once he gets to the big leagues. He sure didn't arrive by underperforming throughout his journey.
- ☆ The real estate agent has displayed the ability to advise clients on buying and selling homes. She had to obtain certain certifications to even be able to practice this type of sale. Even if she doesn't sell a lot of houses over the course of a year, it is not because she lacked the tools necessary to do so, otherwise the agency would have never hired her.
- ☆ The intern who applied to the company passed the screening process and exceled on an interview. He has the tools, based off of the company's evaluation, to produce in this position regardless of what they actually construct.

In each of these instances, the position has already been earned as the tools and skills have been distinguished early on. Therefore, there should be no question about the ability for this person to produce the desired results in the position that they are in. The difficult aspect is to continually produce over the course of a specific time frame. You can't get burnt out along the way or be beaten out by competition within the same industry, team, or company. But as I have mentioned above, this is entirely controlled by the continuous preparation that it takes in order to maintain success. Just because you have graduated to a position that you have desired or have achieved a lifetime goal that you have relentlessly worked for, doesn't mean it's time to become complacent. If you diligently prepared to get to this point, in whatever realm it may be, why would you kick back and relax now? Cruise control shouldn't even be an available function.

In order to stay in this position, you must continue to execute and trust what has allowed you to get to that point. This is what is controllable. This is the preparation that was required. If you think you have made it, and don't think you need to continue to work and operate as if you didn't, you will watch yourself plummet to the level of mediocrity or watch those around you start to rise above your magnitude. This is not because of the idea that you lack skill or don't deserve to be in this position, but because you became complacent and felt as though you have made it. Your production will decrease. Your value will decrease. Your inability to continue to prepare and work becomes your own mechanism of loss. Self-defeat is now your own dispute.

This concept applies to anything you are preparing for. When you don't achieve success, and the self-evaluation process commences, where are your thoughts going to take you? Are you going to play the blame game? Guilt others into thinking it was their fault and make internal excuses as to why you couldn't produce? Or are you going to take responsibility and acknowledge self-defeat as the cause of failure?

- ☆ The major league pitcher who just got demoted to the minor leagues lost his strong work ethic somewhere along the way. He had a little bit of success last year, after relentlessly preparing for the season, and so he expected he would have another year just like it. But this time, he didn't do all the preparation work that originally got him his previous results. He didn't spend time putting in extra hours in the weight room to get stronger and more powerful. He didn't devote any extra energy to arm care and injury prevention. He chose not to log in additional hours of studying opponents before each game. In short, he didn't prepare properly and is forced to suffer the consequences of playing down in the minors.

★ The real estate agent who came in dead last in sales last year is now dealing with the consequences. Not only did she take a financial hit, but it has become harder for her to obtain business. The marketing team doesn't support her as much as the top performers, and she is now last on the list to receive new clients. She must scratch and claw to get back up to par with the rest of the team. The issue was that she became very unorganized in the preparation process of each sale. She was late with paperwork, didn't communicate properly with clients, and didn't do any external research or assistance on her client's behalf. Because of this, many deals fell through. She was great with people, and was more than capable of selling a house, but her preparation didn't permit her to produce.

★ The intern who was hired full time started out successful but has since fallen off the supervisor's leaderboard. His work ethic dropped significantly as he lost focus and became tired of doing work that was unfulfilling. He became miserable, which was evident in his labor. He took no pride in doing *the dirty work* that is often required of junior employees, and therefore was surpassed by those who did.

We can all think of a time when we failed to prepare and therefore had nobody to blame but ourselves. But when this happens the reaction is often to blame others or other factors that could have influenced the result. Deep down, you know you were solely responsible and realize that you could have prevented the failure. But we are not always as self-aware as we should be, especially at younger ages. We also see this lack of self-awareness in a moment where the stakes are high, when preparedness is crucial.

With all this being said, I am hoping that somewhere along the line you have failed and have realized that it was completely your own doing. At some point, especially after failing multiple times at something, you must have looked in the mirror and thought about everything that was done to put yourself in that position.

For me, I was faced with accepting accountability for failing a job interview.

~

I was fresh out of college, still trying to figure out what I wanted to do for a career. I applied for many jobs, even those that I wasn't trained for. Yet, I would apply if I felt as though I would be a good fit.

So, for this one particular job posting, I felt that I had a decent shot at getting it. I applied and passed the background check before advancing to the phone call interview. Once I passed this brief examination, I was then asked to report for an interview that would take place in front of a panel of people.

The morning of the interview I encountered a series of unfortunate events that would eventually lead to my demise. I finished up my morning shift at my part-time job, got dressed, and was planning on shooting straight to the interview facility, which was about forty-five minutes across the border of a neighboring state. As I was getting dressed, I realized that I didn't pack a tie with my suit. I was short on time, so going home to get one wasn't an option, and I really didn't want to risk being late by stopping at a store that would be out of my way. I made the executive decision that I was going to have to interview without a tie and risk being seen as unprofessional. I figured that was better than showing up late.

So, I hopped in the car, plugged the location into my GPS and was on my way. I was about halfway there when I saw the blue lights flashing in the rearview mirror. Although I knew my arrival would be cutting it close, I knew that I wasn't speeding enough to be pulled over, so I was unsure of what was going on. The officer signaled me over to the side and approached my window. "Your right break light is out," he said. "You have to get that fixed as soon as possible." I was relieved that I hadn't done anything wrong and thankful that he then let me go with only a warning. This was good news, but it shook me up. I was trying to get locked in on the interview, but this took my focus elsewhere. Besides, I was now worried about being late.

I pulled up to the building destination with about fifteen minutes to spare, but I now had to find parking. This is always a huge struggle within the city, and I really didn't have time to be roaming the streets in hopes of finding a spot. So, I decided to take a risk and park the car in front of a fire hydrant before hustling into the building.

As you can guess, I was not in the optimal state of mind for an interview at this point in my hectic day. I was likely going to get ticketed and showed up only seconds before the interview, and without a tie, making a poor first impression. Needless to say, my mind was not right.

The interview began, and I cannot even put into words how terribly it went. Like I had mentioned before, it wasn't a job that I was trained for in college, so I didn't know much about it to begin with. And as you can probably guess, I didn't prepare as well as I should have in my research. They asked me basic questions and I countered with ambiguous, shallow answers. At one point, they asked a question, and I couldn't even stir up a response, so we sat there in silence as I tried to come up with something plausible. A few moments later, one of the members of the panel actually asked me if I had learned how to answer these types of questions while in college, a very passive aggressive remark and one that I will never forget. However, at the same time, it had merit. You know it's bad when they start tossing up softball questions just so you can finish the interview. They asked me a final question before abruptly ending the interview after only about twenty minutes, truncating what was supposed to take about an hour. I didn't even make it halfway. And to be quite honest with you, I was in such a fog I can barely recall what they even asked. Anyway, I thanked them for their time when in reality I probably should have apologized for wasting it. They then walked me out and told me they'd be in touch about the next step. We both knew there was no next step. I began walking to my car with a knot in my stomach, knowing that

I had just blown a good opportunity. And to make matters worse, you can guess what happened next. Yup, there it was right on the windshield, a bright pink parking ticket. If this didn't sum up the day, then I don't know what would.

I know I had mentioned in the introduction chapter that the moment in first grade would be the last time I felt unprepared. But obviously, that wasn't the case. I went on to be under-prepared a few more times throughout my younger years. While I was able to grasp the capability of being prepared for daily occurrences early on in my adolescent life, I still hadn't mastered becoming prepared for those big moments. For some, like me, this is much harder to do. For others, they seem to operate disastrously throughout their weekly schedule, but seem to pull it all together for that big moment. Whatever your strength or weakness may be, you need to be able to do both. And if you fail, figure out why.

Through these unprepared moments that have occurred later in my life, I have learned to truly evaluate it for what it's worth. Would I blame others, or would I accept responsibly and then make some conscious decisions to change moving forward? In this instance, on my car ride home, there wasn't anywhere to point the finger:

- ☆ I chose to work that morning instead of taking the extra time to get my mind right.
- ☆ I chose to pack my clothes that morning instead of packing and double checking the night prior.
- ☆ I was the one driving with a break light out. I honestly didn't know it at the time, but I should have. So, I deserved the officer pulling me over.
- ☆ I left many stones unturned in my research of the company and what I was prepared to answer.
- ☆ Self-defeat was now my own dispute.

Failures can lead to future successes. My self-realization of what provoked my poor outcome would become the spur I needed to make sure it never happened again. My next few interviews, and every interview I have had since, have been successful. Not because I am perfect or untouchable, but because I have avoided self-defeat as a result.

We can live with the result when we lose to a better person, team, or company. When you play a perfect game and still lose, all you can do is tip your cap and then dial it back in. It is a much easier pill to swallow than knowing that you beat yourself.

When you review your preparation tactics list, every marker should be checked off and completed, fully. If one tactic is either missed or only partially executed, it can deviate the entire trajectory of your approach. Just like if you shoot a gun at a target with the nose pointing two degrees to the right, that bullet will hit ten feet to the right of the target, proving that even a minor slight can elicit an altered result. If you follow all eight tactics to perfection, and then shortchange the ninth and neglect to get your mind right, the result will be directly influenced. And you can chalk it up to lack of preparedness for leaving potential on the table. If you leave one stone unturned, that could be the information that ultimately holds you back. And when this happens, there is nobody else to blame but yourself.

Self-defeat is the worse type of failure. There is honor in losing to someone who is more capable than you. There is even a level of comfort in knowing that you came up short but exhausted every possible avenue of preparation. But there is no excuse for underperforming when you don't take every actionable, preparatory step. Or maybe that is acceptable to you, but that's a dispute for yourself.

Don't shoot yourself in the foot and then be upset when you can't run.

15
The Feeling of Accomplishment

ONE OF THE greatest sensations resides in the aftermath of accomplishment. This emotion is constructed from the satisfaction in winning, the intrinsic feeling of overcoming, and the recognition of greater value. A feeling so strong, that in the initial moments upon the conclusion, we feel the splendor of raw emotion. During the process, there has been no time or energy devoted to riding the emotional roller coaster. The process has required the commitment to remain level-headed and focused on the long-term goal. So once the outcome has finally been accomplished, there is a sudden moment of relief. An instant where any remaining guard can officially be let down and the sentiment can finally be let out after being pent up for so long.

What does that look like? Michael Jordan on the floor of the locker room sobbing uncontrollably as he holds the NBA finals trophy. The moment a mother delivers her first child and holds the tiny being against her chest. The ensuing moment after you have learned the result of your bar exam and can now obtain your license to practice law. The feeling you get as you look over the mountain range once you have finally reached the summit.

Regardless of how long the process has been to get to this point, the feeling will be universally similar. This rush of excitement floods the body and is too overwhelming for a human to contain. An emotion that gives you the reassurance that everything you have endured along the way has been worth it. This feeling is the result of what you have worked tirelessly for. The sensation provides instant flashbacks of what was encountered throughout the journey. To have overcome obstacles that have been placed in front of you, to have strived to perfect your craft and to have prepared for success are the causes that have led to this exposed emotion.

It is important to note that accomplishment does not only result from the major moment where the lights are shining the brightest. It will also be felt from the completion of the smaller, day-to-day operations that eventually lead to the end goal. Though they hold less significant value and will be overlooked by many, there is satisfaction at the micro level when we are able to take care of system-related goals as we approach the final target. We see this in examples such as:

☆ Having a successful practice, being locked in, and dominating the playing field for that stand alone session.

☆ Completing more chores around the house than you thought you had time for in a given day.

☆ Staying up all night to study the information and going to sleep knowing it will actually make a difference.

In all these instances, there are no immediate feelings of having *made it*; it is an understanding of completing necessary steps to achieve the triumph that has you in tears. It is a symbol of moving in the right direction and therefore gives us a sense of achievement that will only help us keep pushing for more.

The feeling of accomplishment doesn't come from the end product alone. It emerges from the path that it took to get there. This concept is what makes success so desirable, as it forces us to work for it. If you were given a handout or a shortcut to success, you would not experience the feeling of accomplishment. Because you didn't need to embark on a journey of effort, you were therefore not able to develop any type of attachment to it. When unearned, the moment of fruition doesn't inspire any deep level of intimacy toward the accomplishment. It's like cheating on a test; you may have gotten a good grade, but you didn't earn it. This is why, as humans, we love a challenge set out in front of us. Because the mind understands that to detect the true feeling of success, we must endure a process that requires time, commitment, and sacrifice. This sense stems from the ability to toe the line and work for it. Success may in fact reward those who have been given handouts, but they will never be able to feel the same pleasure of truly achieving something they have dedicated themselves to. Simply put, they lack the blood in the game that is required. For them, there was nothing to overcome, therefore, they are left with nothing but an empty, undeserving feeling of success.

Throughout your journey, you will fail more times than you could anticipate. You will be plagued with struggle and difficulty that will occur in different capacities and at different moments. But through this process, you will learn and grow from each individual experience that will only shape you into a person who is destined for success. When you get knocked down, or face a setback, you will stand back up, dust yourself off and then re-engage. The end goal will also require monotonous work and repetitive actions that don't necessarily yield results right away. This can be demoralizing, especially if the process is prolonged, so think back to the story of the ax and the tree. Nobody will chop the tree down in one swing; it demands the same repetitive strike over and over again. This process acts in the same way as it demands diligent and strong mental fortitude along the way, especially during times where results aren't tangible. It is the faith and belief in what you are doing that keeps you moving forward. And when you finally accomplish success, you will instantly be reminded of all the repetitions that seemed meaningless at the time, but eventually led to the current moment you are experiencing.

In short, here's how accomplishment works:

> **You begin with a vision of a desired outcome. The process of developing an organized plan, uncovering a path, and then getting to work will then quickly ensue. Along the way, you design your road map to success; you will then be challenged**

to become disciplined in your execution. There will be alternate routes that project themselves and constant distractions along the way where you will need to rely on discipline to keep you aligned. Commitment, repetitive work, and sacrifice are essential components that will keep you on a clear path to your goal. From here on out, you will only engage in ways that promote perfection and rely on both your mental and physical qualities. Pretty soon, you will find yourself closing in on that goal of yours, and when the process to achieve success is completed, the sense of accomplishment is therefore merited. Sounds familiar, right?

That's because your preparation is the prime reason for that feeling of accomplishment you experience when you achieve success. What you endure is responsible for the raw emotions you will undergo when the process is successfully completed. You will reflect on everything that you have done along the way. You will remember areas where you made yourself *get organized*, the countless hours you spent *visualizing the moment* of success, of leaving *no stone unturned* in your approach to what needs to get done, and then *starting right away* to begin the journey.

You will recollect on the time it took to *become disciplined* and the energy it required to become fully *committed to the process*, the repeated actions that were put together in order to *make it a habit*, and your ability to be *willing to sacrifice* various other life events and outside factors that could potentially get in the way.

Finally, you will recall the pressure it took to *pursue perfection*, the mindset that it took to be *about the dirty work*, the constant quest for perfection where you looked to eliminate error by *aiming high* and therefore *missing high* in your execution, and then the mental capacity to *get your mind right* in the moments leading up to impact. Your preparation is responsible for the outcome.

The feeling of accomplishment is so substantial because, by doing all this, you develop a direct relationship with both the expedition and the final product. You can appreciate the moment much more when you can reflect on what you have been through to get there.

It took Michael Jordan seven years of struggle and failure before he was able to experience the celebration of an NBA championship. It takes the mother nine months of discomfort before welcoming the gift of a child. It takes seven years of college and months of intensive studying to pass the bar exam. It takes hours of grueling, repetitive steps for the hiker to reach the summit and experience a view of a lifetime.

When all is said and done, you will be able to look back and be proud of what you were willing to do to succeed. Your drive to prepare yourself, withstand the work and steer your actions into positive results; that's what the process is about. This is what makes the end goal so desirable and worth it in the end. The obstacles, struggles, and bouts of adversity are what make the level of appreciation so immense. Instead of quitting, or being too afraid to even begin, you ran toward the goal and didn't let anything stop you. When others doubted you or spewed their negativity onto you, you didn't entertain it for a second. You passed the test both physically and mentally to earn the recognition, in whatever capacity it may be. You have earned the right to soak in the overwhelming feeling of achievement.

Your ability to experience one of the best feelings a human can experience is entirely dependent on your ability to prepare. When you lack in this department, failure will shortly ensue, and you will be left at the altar with no understanding of what it may be like to accomplish something. But when you prepare, and therefore earn everything that is coming your way, you will bask in the moment of realization. The sense of achievement can only be understood by those willing to fully prepare, and as a result, succeed.

As humans, we all crave the result of success, but what most don't realize is that it is only temporary. Pretty soon, somebody else will come in and take your spot. Somebody else will go a little bit higher than you were able to go. We see this all the time as athletic records are broken, new people are hired, and standards are continually raised. However, the feeling of accomplishment lasts forever.

When you endure what nobody else is willing to, or when you experience a process that is utterly dependent on your performance— without shortcuts or handouts— you have earned the right to feel the way that you do. Few are willing to do what it takes to experience this kind of pleasure, but when you prepare with this level of relentlessness, you naturally develop the ability to sustain it. The bond of work becomes networked, creating a degree of attachment that is hardwired into you. And when there is direct attachment to the process, the feeling of accomplishment is therefore warranted.

CONCLUSION
You are in Control

WHAT YOU HAVE probably already figured out, and most likely had before you even decided to pick up this book, is that I am not some famous figure with an enormous platform. I understand that this can persuade how you receive the material, especially in today's world that is filled with social media fame and popularity. In this lifestyle, we all can gain access to knowledge in any field, and at any given moment. While this is great for the world, it can also be just as detrimental. You see, because of this new landscape in the digital space, it has become easier than ever to gain fame.

As we stand today, controversy is the name of the game. With that comes a lot of false narratives and people who are looking to gain clout by standing outside of the norm. With these platforms, people can say and make claims to anything that they want. With that comes a lot of bullshit, but because it may be different from what everybody else says or does, it gains attraction. Once you have attention, it is then easy to continue to attract that crowd of people who you have already duped. I would just advise you to be cognizant of your sources and where you place your attention. This will force you to be diligent in your research and require you to have the intelligence to filter falsities as you acquire new knowledge.

I wanted to create a book with material that drives results. As you can tell, I have not created any magic pill to success, nor have I claimed to be the preparation guru in any way. I am not looking for clout and am certainly not trying to be controversial. But what I have tried to do is simply lay out a proven blueprint of tactics that I have used, and have watched others use, to become better prepared individuals. The results from these practices have been colossal both for me, and the people I have watched use them. Additionally, as you can tell, I purposely did not leave you with any groundbreaking information. The art of preparing is simple, and my goal is to provide you with the tools to put the simplistic principles to practice. The toughest part, and always will be the toughest part, is for you to then drop the book and start executing. This is why I have provided a tactical list that can be consistently reviewed for reference.

The information in this book has all been acquired through my own life. The content is based around knowledge that I have learned from the professional and collegiate athletes with whom I have worked, the adolescents and the adult clients who I have trained, the populations I have been immersed in while attaining multiple degrees at numerous universities, staffs I have been a part of, places and cultures I have experienced, and so on. Nothing I have discussed is meant to be the perfect solution for anybody, and I am certainly not claiming that following these tactics guarantees success for everyone.

What I can promise is that by learning and then implementing the material in this book, you can change the trajectory of your life. The results from the big moments go without saying. You will ace those tests, crush those presentations, and dominate those games. By following these tactics, you set yourself up for full control of every scenario, positioning you to reap the rewards. But what I hope to make even more of an impact on, and what I believe will come as a surprise, is improvements to your daily quality of life. You will no longer be the person to show up late, forget an assignment, or be cluttered with extra activity and tasks that distract you from important duties. You will transform how you shape your days and program your weeks. And as a result, you will then reap the rewards of being prepared for every curveball life throws at you.

You will take back full control of your decisions, your actions, and your overall life. People will take notice, but even more importantly, you will feel the difference. Tasks soon start to become easier as you become more organized. You can accomplish more as you commit and remain disciplined throughout the process. You will execute to perfection in the actions that you take. Excuses are no longer permitted as everything becomes entirely up to you and how you prepare.

When you can make this transformation, you become visible through an entirely different lens. There is no denying that the person in the office or within the organization who seems to have all their stuff in order radiates an unmatched energy. This person has a presence about them that comes off as desirable and wise. This is the type of person that if you want to confront, you better have solid case because you know they understand all their surroundings and everything that has taken place. You will never catch them off guard. From the way that they walk, to the body posture they present when they enter a room, to the hours they clock in and out, to the way they hold conversations, everything is entirely methodical. You will never have to question this person because they are completely dependable. Nothing ever slips the cracks or goes without completion. They have their life entirely under control, which makes them very appealing. Everything is about efficiency, and as a result, their production and reputation within the company catapults. This is who I hope you can become.

Sweat more during peace, bleed less during war is just a saying to some, but to many has become a lifestyle. I hope after reading this book, you will live by the principles of this deeper meaning. You and the world around you will surely benefit from it. We need more people who have their lives under control. The world is calling for those who don't make excuses for controllable actions. We need more organized and diligent counterparts. And we need more people who prepare with the purpose to create results instead of waiting for life to dictate their fate. The good news is that the change can begin with you, so I challenge you to take these tactics and put them to use. It's time for you to be in control.

THE TACTICAL PLAN OF PREPARATION

Get Organized

    Tactic 1...Visualize the Moment
    Tactic 2...Start Right Away
    Tactic 3...Leave No Stone Unturned

Become Disciplined

    Tactic 4...Commit to the Process
    Tactic 5...Make it a Habit
    Tactic 6...Be Willing to Sacrifice

Pursue Perfection

    Tactic 7...Be About the Dirty Work
    Tactic 8...Aim High, Miss High
    Tactic 9...Get Your Mind Right

ACKNOWLEDGMENTS

WRITING THIS BOOK has been a joy. For what just began as my own thoughts and philosophies, which have now become my own words that are shared with the world, the writing process has truly been a privilege. I would love to first list off all the publishers and agents who passed on this work, because you really only inspired me to press forward. But more importantly, I want to thank those who believed in me.

To my mom and dad, thank you for raising me the way that you did. Everything I have accomplished in this life is a direct result from the lessons and qualities that you have instilled in me. You have always been my biggest supporters and words cannot give my gratitude any justice.

Thank you to my wife who has been my support through this entire process. When most people would have thought I was joking about writing a book, you believed in it from the start.

To the rest of my family and close friends, thank you for everything you have done for me along the way. You have always been there for me, and I will never take that for granted.

Thank you to the mentors, coaches, and colleagues whom I have had the privilege of working alongside of. I hope you learn from this book a fraction of what I have been able to learn from each of you.

To anybody who was indirectly mentioned in this book, thank you for providing me with lessons that have truly stuck with me. From teachers to classmates, business professionals to other authors, thank you for inspiring the stories in this book.

Thank you to all the agents and publishers who took the time to read, provide feedback, and see the value in my original manuscript. It was the few of you who made me feel as though I could call myself an author.

And finally, a special thank you to all the athletes that I have had the privilege of coaching. You inspire me every single day and have pushed me to become both a better person and coach. Without each of you, this book would have never been a thought.

www.ingramcontent.com/pod-product-compliance
Lightning Source LLC
LaVergne TN
LVHW041845070526
838199LV00045BA/1441